Jan 1988

To

Tin Smith

in hope we meet

Mcleod Kenny

THINK about
Terrorism

The New Warfare

Terrell E. Arnold and Moorhead Kennedy
The THINK Series

Walker and Company
720 Fifth Ave.
New York City, NY 10019

Figure 4 courtesy of the Library of Congress; Figures 6, 21 by permission of AP/Wideworld Photo; Figures 14, 18 official photo courtesy of the U.S. Air Force; Figures 16, 17 Copyright the Washington Post: reprinted by permission of the D.C. Public Library

First published in the United States of America in 1988 by the Walker Publishing Company, Inc.

Published simultaneously in Canada by Thomas Allen & Son Canada, Limited, Markham, Ontario.

Library of Congress Cataloging-in-Publication Data

Arnold, Terrell E.
  Think about terrorism: motivations, methods, and responses
Terrell E. Arnold and Moorhead Kennedy.
      p.   cm.—(The Think series)
  Bibliography: p.
  Includes index.
  Summary: Discusses various aspects of international terrorism, how it affects our lives, and possible solutions to this escalating problem.
  ISBN 0-8027-6757-5.   ISBN 0-8027-6758-3 (pbk.)
  1. Terrorism—Juvenile literature
  2. Terrorism—Prevention—
Juvenile literature.   [1. Terrorism.]   I. Kennedy, Moorhead.
II. Title.   III. Series.
HV6431.A76 1988
303.6'25—dc19   87-21158
                      CIP
                      AC

Printed in the United States of America

10 9 8 7 6 5 4 3 2 1

ACKNOWLEDGEMENTS

To the Myrin Institute, and, in particular to Marion and Olivia Gilliam who encouraged this book, my thanks. Also to Rosannah Cole, whose skill with the wordprocessor made it possible. And to Martha Keys, the initiator of the simulation, 'Hostage Crisis,' which will continue the learning experience begun by this book.

The authors and the publisher acknowledge the significant contribution of Laura Reynolds. Her assistance in researching and writing this book as part of the staff of the Institute on Terrorism was invaluable.

The THINK Series' Editors: William N. Thorndike Jr., Ramsey R. Walker

Stylistic editor: Jo Basham
Fact checker: Louise Benton
Reding consultants: Ann-Marie Longo, Paula Sable

Jacket design: Joyce C. Weston
Text design: Joyce C. Weston
Photo research: Diane Hamilton
Graphs: Jill Thompson
Jacket illustration: Tom Hughes
Text illustrations: Jeff Danziger
Appendix A written by J. B. Schramm

The editors would like to thank the many teachers, librarians and students that assisted in putting together the THINK Series. It would be impossible to thank everybody; however, we would especially like to thank the following people: John Buckey, Betty Carter, Jim Davis, Mike Hartoonian, Tedd Levy, David Mallery, Mike Printz, Bill Polk, Mary Tabor, Ellen Ramsey.

To those who go abroad
to serve their country.

CONTENTS

1 Introduction

What is terrorism?
Why do we need to know more about it?
How do we define it?
What more will we need to know?

WHAT IS TERRORISM?

Almost every day we read or hear about a terrorist attack somewhere. The attacks have grown in number during the 1980s. They now affect our people, our country, and our interests in almost every part of the world. Terrorism affects us personally, because people we know get hurt, killed, or taken hostage. We realize that it can happen to us, although the chances are small.

Let's start our study of this unique kind of warfare by looking at some specific terrorist incidents.

Incident 1. In June 1985, two hooded hijackers took over TWA Flight 847 as it departed from Athens, Greece. Shortly after the takeover, the hijackers demanded passports from passengers and began to study them. From information they got from the passports, they singled out a young American, U.S. Navy frogman Robert Stethem, and took him into the

1

cockpit. There, they beat him, and finally they shot him.

Incident 2. On November 4, 1979, the American Embassy in Tehran, Iran, was invaded and taken over by Iranians who called themselves Students in the Path of the Imam. As told by one of the authors, Moorhead Kennedy, "Our people soon found out that the Iranian government was not going to send police to help them. They had to surrender to these religious revolutionaries, who tied their hands behind their backs and blindfolded them." Soon, with fifty other Americans, Moorhead Kennedy was taken to a house outside the city to begin a captivity which lasted 444 days. In various groups, the hostages were held until January 20, 1981, when arrangements finally were worked out with the Ayatollah Khomeini, Iran's religious ruler, to let our hostages return home.

Incident 3. In May 1984 a Tamil separatist group in Sri Lanka kidnapped a young American couple and

Figure 1—Ayatollah Khomeini, Iran's religious leader, led the revolution in that country during which the Americans were held hostage for 444 days.

held them prisoner for five days. The aim of this group was to put pressure on the govenment of Sri Lanka to split off the northern part of Sri Lanka and to create an independent Tamil state. Late one night, Terry Arnold received a telephone call from the American ambassador in Colombo, who said, "Terry, nothing is happening. Do you have any thoughts on what is going on?" Terry said, "The terrorists have not renewed their demand for money and they have not made any new demands. I think that means they are running down; they are looking for a way to end this incident without getting themselves caught." The next day the terrorists delivered their hostages unharmed to the home of a bishop in the town of Jaffna. The terrorists then got quickly away.

The incidents you have just read about are the first of many we will use in this book to help show you different aspects of terrorist activity. All the cases you will study are true stories, chosen to illustrate points about terrorism.

What are the basic points made by these cases? Each incident is very different. Each occurred in a different region of the world. Each involved terrorists with very different goals, yet each case affected Americans and American interests.

Keep these points in mind as we go on with our study: In the 1980's, according to U.S. statistics, the number of international terrorist attacks has risen sharply, from an average of about five hundred per year to almost 750 per year in 1986. While we see much more in our media about terrorist attacks in Europe and the Middle East, many attacks occur in Latin America and sub-Saharan Africa as well. There

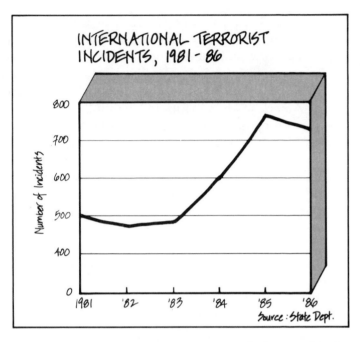

INTERNATIONAL TERRORIST INCIDENTS, 1981-86

Number of Incidents

800
700
600
500
400
0

1981   '82   '83   '84   '85   '86

Source: State Dept.

are some attacks in every region of the world. In many different ways, terrorism affects national policy, not only for the United States, but for most countries. Look at the millions of dollars governments now spend to provide physical security for embassies and for people. Terrorism affects people's personal plans, too: In 1986 more than a million Americans who planned trips to Europe did not make their trips. Of course, hostages and their families also often undergo deeply traumatic experiences.

Because of the dramatic increase in terrorist attacks and the effects of those attacks on Americans, on America's allies, and on American interests, we must learn as much as possible about terrorism and its causes.

In beginning our study of terrorism, we will look first at the U.S. government's definition of terrorism. Then, to help you flesh out your understanding of terrorism, we will explore the following questions:

- Why do terrorists do what they do?
- Who are the terrorists?
- How do they do what they do?
- Where?
- Who are their targets?

The answers to these questions will give you the background you need to think about the important issues raised by the growing use of terrorism. Some of these questions include the following:

- What is the proper role of media?
- What can governments do about terrorism?
- What can *you* do about terrorism?

You need answers to all these questions. As citizens, *your* ideas are important. The president and the Congress, those who will be making the basic decisions about terrorism, will be elected by you. All of us need to examine problems such as:

- How to protect our embassies, business personnel, and ordinary citizens who travel to foreign countries.
- How to make sure that travel in our own country is safe.
- How to defend ourselves, and to help others defend themselves.
- How to understand terrorist's grievances, and why terrorists consider them important enough to commit violent acts.

- How to deal with those grievances without resort to violence, if possible.

A BASIC DEFINITION

Many people argue that you cannot define terrorism. They use catchy phrases, like "One man's terrorist is another man's freedom fighter," implying that there is no single definition. But that is simply taking the

Figure 3—Defining terrorism is not an easy task. Are the Contras fighting in Nicaragua freedom fighters or terrorists? Some people might consider a group as terrorist while other people would consider the same group freedom fighters.

easy way out. In our study we must work harder than that to see if we can identify the main qualities that make terrorism different from other kinds of violence.

We need as clear a meaning for the word "terrorism" as possible, so that we can talk sensibly with other people about it. A good definition will help to protect us from other people's abuses of language. As individuals we cannot make sound decisions— and our government cannot make sound policies— without a definition of terrorism that we all find acceptable.

In its February 1986 report, the Vice President's Task Force on Terrorism defined terrorism this way:

> Terrorism "is the unlawful use or threat of violence against persons or property to further political or social objectives. It is generally intended to intimidate or coerce a government, individuals or groups to modify their behavior or policies. The terrorist's methods may include hostage-taking, aircraft piracy or sabotage, assassination, threats, hoaxes, indiscriminate bombings or shootings."

Stripped down to essentials, this definition has three main parts. Part one says that *terrorism is* the "use or threat of violence" to promote a "political or social" goal. Part two says that *the aim of terrorism is* to "intimidate or coerce a government, individuals or groups" to change their "behavior or policies." Part three says that *the common methods of terrorism are* "hostage-taking, aircraft piracy or sabotage, assassination," and other forms of violence or threats of violence.

As you can see already, defining terrorism is no

simple matter. There are several different elements to consider, and these elements correspond to our earlier list of questions: Why? Who? How? Where? To whom? Answers to these questions will give us a broad understanding of terrorism. We can then look at ways to respond, both personally and on a national level.

REVIEW QUESTIONS

1. Has the number of terrorist incidents been rising or falling in recent years?
2. What questions should we ask to get a full understanding of terrorism?
3. What is the Vice President's Task Force on Terrorism's definition of terrorism?

2 | The Reasons for Terrorism

Why do terrorists do what they do?
Do terrorists act because of a single reason, or a combination of reasons?
Are the reasons terrorists give for their actions always the real reasons for those actions?

To understand better why terrorists do what they do, we need to look at their *motives*. Terrorist motives fall into three main classes:

1. To promote various causes, such as a nation, a religion, or ideology, or an ethnic tradition or culture. These are often the "public" reasons terrorists give to explain or justify their behavior to themselves and to others.
2. To satisfy inner feelings and emotions—violence, revenge, anger, disappointment, fear, and personal inadequacy.
3. To pursue personal drives—greed, power, desire for professional success or recognition, and security.

People generally operate from a mixture of motives. The terrorist is no exception. Before reaching any judgments about terrorist groups or individuals, try

9

to determine the motivating forces. This is difficult because the terrorist rarely tells you about his inner feelings or emotions or drives. What you usually see and hear is the "public" justification of the terrorist. Still, it is worthwhile to try to find the real motives, for then realistic and effective policies can be followed.

NATIONALISM

As Americans from many different races, creeds, cultures, and national origins, we have strong feelings about our country, its flag, its proud history, and its influence in the world today. Such feelings make up what we call **nationalism.** Peoples who do not have a country of their own, however, or who have no established loyalty to one, may still have strong group or nationalistic feelings. For example, Jewish nationalistic feelings, based on remembrance of a homeland lost since biblical times, survived over centuries when Jews lacked a common geographical location, statehood, or government. Many Jews rediscovered these key elements when they returned from many parts of the world, mainly from Europe and other Middle East countries, to Palestine to establish the modern State of Israel. Palestinians who live, or used to live, in historic Palestine, part of which is now Israel, have equally strong nationalistic feelings, made even stronger because they sense that they are not able to regain their homeland, or to enjoy independence or statehood in some part of it.

Terrorism is one means resorted to by people who seek to regain or to create a homeland for themselves. For example, the **Palestine Liberation Organization,** or **PLO,** argues that unless they "play the terrorist card," the rest of the world will not pay attention to their demand for a homeland and a state of their own. Using very similar arguments, such Jewish terrorist groups as the Irgun zvai Leumi and the Sternists set out shortly after the end of World War II to force the withdrawal of the British authorities who govern Palestine. These groups also forced the flight of much of the Palestinian population in order to pave the way for the establishment of the State of Israel. Ever since, terrorism has made victims of many Israelis and Palestinians. People on both sides have been killed or injured, and the communities have been dissolved during the almost four-decade-long cycle of violence.

Other groups seeking to establish or preserve a homeland include Armenians, Kurds, Croatians, Basques, Tamils of Sri Lanka, numerous tribal groups in Africa, and a number of tribal groups in North, Central, and South America. In order to remind others that they exist and what their demands are, or in hopes of forcing agreement to their demands, terrorists from some of these groups may go to extreme lengths. During the Christmas shopping season in London in 1983, the Irish Republican Army, which calls for the unification of Ireland, planted a bomb outside a major department store. In India on October 31, 1984, Sikh separatists, who want to carve their own state out of India and want the freedom to practice their religion, assassinated the Indian prime minister, Indira Gandhi.

Many terrorist groups claim to speak for an entire nation. Not all the people within the same country or geographic area, however, may agree with the terror-

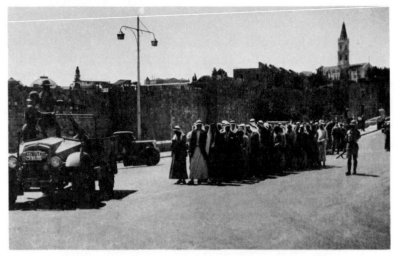

Figure 4—Nationalism is one of the most common motives for terrorist incidents, especially in the Middle East, where a combination of nationalist and religious conflict has occurred at an increasing rate for many decades. This photo shows Palestinians under temporary arrest in 1938 after a rebellion against the growth of Jewish settlement.

ists. Some groups within a country may have been enemies for centuries. Sometimes, because the area is very small, or because the hostile groups are not living in separate areas, the country cannot be subdivided in ways that satisfy each group. Sometimes, as in the case of Palestine after World War II, several groups end up trying to control the same territory. Historic Palestine, as remembered by the Palestinian people, has been occupied since World War II by Israel, Egypt, and Jordan. The Palestinians control no part of it. Thus, the attempt by some Palestinians to regain their homeland takes the form of terrorist activity.

Different groups within a country may also disagree about its future. Some may want to break away from the larger country and form their own, independent country. Others may want nothing more than the right to use their own language, or enjoy local self-government.

In judging the claims of any terrorist group to *legitimacy* (which means deciding whether you accept their goal, as well as their *right* to seek it), you will first have to recognize that many of these situations are very complex, and that many of them relate to the interests of several parties. Each group or organization involved may present what sounds like a good case. Before you reach any judgment, you will want to learn as much as you can about these groups, their backgrounds and histories, their goals, and their practices.

RELIGION AND IDEOLOGY

Many terrorists justify their actions and goals by referring to religion or ideology. An *ideology* is a set of beliefs, in some ways like religion, which people use to create an idea of how the world should run and how people should behave in it. They then compare this model against the world as it is. They also teach and promote ways to make the world like their model.

One main difference between religion and ideology is that an ideology does not necessarily include the idea of God, or of a supreme being. Communism or Marxism is one example of an ideology. **Anarchism,** the belief that all government is unnecessary and undesirable, is another ideology.

In contrast to Marxists and **anarchists,** who at least

have a model for what they consider to be a better world, many ideological terrorists are largely negative in their focus. That is, they may be dedicated to getting rid of rulers or systems that they consider unjust. However, these terrorists often lack ideas, or entertain fuzzy ones at best, about the kind of system or ruler that they would like in replacement. More often than not, they lack practical solutions for the injustices of which they complain. Most destructive of all ideological terrorists are **nihilists,** those who maintain that traditional beliefs and values have no foundation, and that life itself is senseless and useless. Many consider the terrorrist group, the Red Army Faction, also known as the Baader-Meinhaf Gang, to be nihilists.

Terrorists who base their actions on religion or ideology often argue their case with statements like these:

- My beliefs are right.
- I can therefore use force or any other means to make you accept my ideas.
- I will not compromise my ideas to make them more acceptable to you.
- Those who share my beliefs are friends.
- Those who oppose my beliefs are enemies.
- Those who stand in the way are enemies.
- To attack those enemies is a good thing.
- Since I am right and you are wrong, I do not have to consider any of your arguments or beliefs, even if that means we never resolve our differences, or end up in a bloody quarrel.

We list these statements because they are basic to the thinking of the **fanatic.** Fanatics are those whose belief in a cause is so strong that they will not look closely at their own motives or consider anybody else's rights and interests. Religious fanatics are particularly dangerous, because they are convinced that their God is telling them what to do. Believing, under their religion, that entrance into an afterlife is made easier by dying in the fight for their religion, a few terrorists have become very dangerous and even suicidal. Terrorists who believe that their ideology is a better way can also become fanatical, prepared to risk or lose their lives for their cause. The Lebanese **Shiite** who, in 1983, drove a truck laden with dynamite into a U.S. Marine barracks near the Beirut International Airport, thereby killing 241 marines, was said to be a fanatic. But not very many terrorists are suicidal fanatics. While most terrorists are prepared to take risks, they still spend much of their time trying to stay alive.

Figure 5—Many terrorists assume that they are on the side of right against wrong, good against evil.

Some terrorists believe that their God is on the side of their country, their people, or their political cause—against another country, people, or political cause. Often, they identify their religious group with their country. Both are part of the terrorist identity. In many areas of the world people identify more closely with their religious, cultural, or ethnic community than they do with the country whose flag they salute.

To illustrate, in parts of the Middle East, of Pakistan, and of East Asia, a number of Muslims contend that **Islam,** in a rigorous form, should take the place of the modern nation-state and the values and practices of the West. This "**Islamic** fundamentalism" has been adopted by many Palestinians, who contend that the loss of their homeland to the Israelis was the consequence of a weakening of their religious faith. In the words of an Israeli expert, these **fundamentalists** are "reaffirming their identity as Muslims, above all else, and aspiring to liberate Palestine as a Muslim land." Iran under the Ayatollah Khomeini is now an Islamic republic, governed according to fundamentalist Islamic principles. **Shiism,** the kind of Islam practiced in Iran, is also practiced by the majority of Lebanese Muslims. Taking advantage of this connection, the Iranian government supports the most violent of Lebanon's Shiite groups. Thus religion, rather than nationalism, is used by Khomeini to link up with fundamentalists outside Iran and to promote terrorism through them.

ETHNIC BACKGROUND AND CULTURE

Among terrorism's many motives, one relates to a process we all go through. It is the process of growing up, part of which is finding out who you are. Another part is letting your friends, your relations, and your parents know that you are a person in your own right. You want them to understand the changes that you are going through and to respect you as the person you are, or the person you are trying to become.

Many people in the developing countries of the world are going through a similar "growing-up" process. These countries are trying now to establish their sense of identity. In some cases we are talking about very old countries, often going back thousands of years. In many other cases, we are talking about groups or tribes which have never really been countries but are seeking to establish an identity as a group or people who control their own territory.

People trying to establish or reestablish their identities often feel that their culture, their identity, is threatened by outside influences. A number of developing countries feel that way. They fear the influences of foreign cultures for three reasons:

1. Everywhere they look in their countries, they see evidence of the influence of foreign cultures. Their TV channels and movie houses feature foreign films, their bookstores carry foreign books and magazines. They worry that the way they think is being erased by alien thoughts; they fear that they are becoming foreigners in their own countries and that they are forgetting who they really are. In other words, they are having an *identity crisis*. This kind of a crisis is very unsettling to the individual. It can shake a country as well.
2. The value systems of Western cultures also worry

people in developing countries. First, they worry about the appeal that these cultures hold for their young people and for their most ambitious and best trained people. They consider many of their own values to be superior to those of Western cultures, but they fear their values will be lost in collision with the attractions of the West. Western influences will undermine their own values, they feel. For example, Western sexual freedom shocks fundamentalist Muslims. The Iranian revolution ordered that young men and young women shouldn't even sit in the same classroom together.

3. Many critics in developing countries also consider the way the world economy is organized to be wasteful and greedy, designed to serve rich countries and individuals at the expense of the poor.

It is difficult for people in developing countries to counter Western influences and to establish or restore their own sense of identity. The openness of the world community makes it easy for foreign ideas to enter. Techniques for resisting and expelling these influences are few. Some think that one technique is terrorism.

Techniques for Maintaining Ethnicity and Culture

Although it is a difficult task, some countries do attempt to maintain their culture and value systems in the face of Western influence. Several examples follow.

Reasserting Traditional Practices. The Islamic religious revolution that took over Iran in January 1979 was welcomed by many Iranians. They hoped that a society dominated by their traditional religion would make them feel more Iranian and less "Western." The leader of the revolution, the Ayatollah Khomeini, had practical ways to remind Iranians of their identity. For example, he ordered that the American-style toilets in a big resort hotel be taken out and replaced by Iranian-style toilets, with two places for your feet and a hole in the floor. Westerners wondered why Khomeini, the religious leader and political head of his country, worried about something like toilets? When Moorhead Kennedy was taken hostage and volunteered to swab out the Western-style washroom in the U.S. Embassy, which were also used by the guards, he learned why. He had to clean the guards' footprints off the toilet seats. They preferred this way because that was their toilet training. Such things become part of a person's identity. Khomeini, trying to break the links of the West to Iran, saw the toilet as one important place to begin.

Expelling Foreign Influences. The Ayatollah Khomeini argues that all foreign influences should be expelled from the Middle East, because he fears that they will undermine his fundamentalist revolution. For this reason he has helped terrorists attack sources of foreign influence. Consider the jobs of the Americans who were held or killed in Lebanon by Shiite Muslim religious fundamentalists. The list includes:

- the president of the American University of Beirut (AUB)—murdered
- the vice president of AUB—held hostage and then released

- the administrator of AUB Hospital—held hostage and then released
- the dean of agriculture at AUB—still being held hostage as of this writing
- the librarian of AUB—held hostage and then executed
- three faculty members from Beirut University College (an American institution)—still held hostage as of this writing
- the principal of an American private school in Beirut—still held hostage as of this writing
- a Roman Catholic priest—held hostage and then released
- a Presbyterian missionary—held hostage and then released
- the bureau chief in Beirut of the Associated Press—still held hostage as of this writing
- the bureau chief in Beirut of Cable News Network—held hostage and escaped
- a television reporter for ABC—taken hostage in June 1987 and then escaped.

Do you see the reason these people were taken hostage? They are all *communicators:* people who, in one way or another, have been spreading Western culture and outside influences in the Middle East.

Reminding Others of Differences. Just as you want your friends, parents, and teachers to understand why you are unique, people in many parts of the world want others to understand who they are. They want people to be aware of the changes they are going through, and to recognize why they want to

Figure 6—Demonstrators carry a banner with an anti-American message as they march on Tehran, December 11, 1978. An estimated one million demonstrators took part in the march.

preserve and protect their own values, traditions, and cultures.

Moorhead Kennedy recalls that when he appeared on a TV program with Hossein Sheikholeslam, a leader and spokesman of Kennedy's former captors in 1984, he asked Sheikholeslam what his student group had hoped to gain by taking over the U.S. Embassy. The Iranian, today Deputy Foreign Minister of Iran, replied that when he had been a student in the United States, most Americans did not know where Iran was. But after the Embassy takeover, he said, "most of the American people know where Iran is . . . and what Iran stands for."

Trying to Have It Both Ways. Many in the Third World do not want Western influences to stop altogether. They admire our lifestyles. They need our technology and our professional skills. Even as some of them hate and fear the influence of our culture and its technology, many realize that they may need Western help to defend themselves. Moorhead Kennedy recalls a room where his captors had placed on the wall a poster which read, "America, get out of our country, get out of our region." He said to a guard, "The Soviets are invading Afghanistan. What will you do if the Soviets do to Iran what they are doing to Afghanistan?" The guard replied, "Oh, you would have to come to our defence. We are too important to you." Kennedy realized right away that what the Iranian was *really* saying was, "*You* are too important to *us*."

Some terrorists are motivated by their desire to protect their ethnic and cultural identities from threatening outside influences. Sometimes, to do this, they restore traditional practices. Sometimes they try to frighten away those who spread foreign influences. Sometimes they remind themselves and others of their own different ideas and political positions. At the same time, they want to keep some connection with the West.

VIOLENCE AS A MOTIVATING FORCE

Terrorists can be very violent—women as well as men. For some, violence is a motivation in itself. These individuals are drawn into terrorism as a way to practice violence. Other terrorists practice violence out of fear for their own safety. Especially when something goes wrong with their plan, terrorists can suddenly turn violent, striking out at those who refuse to cooperate. Some of the violence, of course, is used in order to frighten their victims into submission or to gain more attention for their cause.

Terrorists often argue that their reasons for using violence are to support some good cause—to bring an end to violations of human rights, for example, or to achieve the independence of their country from foreign rule. Some claim to seek justice and fair treatment for all people. But in pursuing those stated objectives, they often perform cruel and inhuman acts that deny justice to others, particularly to the people they kill, injure, kidnap, or frighten.

Making sense out of this conflict of signals—terrorists who say they have high ideals, but who kill, injure, and confine innocent people—is not easy for the terrorists or for their victims. It can be bewildering for hostages, who never know when their captors are going to perform some violent act or when they may display gentle or even caring behavior. Moorhead Kennedy remembers one guard who expressed sympathy for one of the hostages who was depressed. The same guard said, however, "Don't ever forget, we can keep you tied to chairs for the rest of your time with us, or we can kill you."

Some terrorists are motivated by the personal satisfaction they find in violence. Some become violent when frightened or frustrated. Some act violently for effect. Many have problems reconciling their ideals with the violent acts they perform.

REVENGE

Some terrorists try to excuse violent behavior by calling it an act of *revenge*. Remember the killing of U.S. Navy frogman Robert Stethem, which we cited earlier? The immediate demand of the terrorists who killed Robert Stethem was to get more than six hundred Shiite Muslims out of captivity in Israel. To further justify their attack, the killers said that they were taking revenge for the shelling of their villages in Lebanon by the U.S. Navy, an action designed to protect the U.S. marines who were engaged on a peacekeeping mission in that country.

Consider this final example of a so-called revenge action. Many Turkish diplomats have been assassinated by Armenian terrorist groups. Others, including Americans, have been victims of Armenian terrorist attacks. These groups argue that they are trying to force the Turkish government to admit to and apologize for mass killings of Armenians by a Turkish government that was overthrown more than sixty years ago.

POWER

Brian Jenkins, a leading authority on terrorism, once observed that "terrorism is about being in control, (about) having power." The goals and objectives that we have examined, such as independence, expelling foreign influences, or much more modest objectives, require that terrorists find some way to influence events. Either they acquire power on their own, or they need the help of influential groups or states.

Besides being a means to bring about changes, power can be an important drive in itself. In terrorists, who put themselves in danger for their causes, the power drive becomes particularly strong. As evidence of this, look at what happens to many terrorists who once asserted that they were dedicated to human rights and the democratic process. Often, after they have achieved the power they seek, they become more dictatorial, more abusive of human rights, than the rulers they have displaced. Fidel Castro, the dictatorial ruler in Cuba, or the Sandinistas in Nicaragua, were themselves once in rebellion against dictatorial governments. Today, they commit many of the same abuses against which they once protested.

Because their individual power drives are so strong, terrorists are often deeply distrustful of one another's ambitions, and fearful that others will misuse power if it is given to them. This explains why, in quest of power or because of suspicion of others, terrorist leaders and groups will often attack other groups or even their own members. Recent examples include attacks by the Irish National Liberation Army on other **factions** of the IRA, and by Palestinian groups on one another.

FEAR, SECURITY, AND THE GROUP

Security is a major drive of terrorists. In fact, in small, tightly-knit groups, security becomes almost an obsession. The Iran hostages for several months lacked hot water in the building where they were kept because their captors did not dare bring in a plumber, who might learn too much. The same captors' security committee appears to have become most important among ruling committees, because it was responsible for protecting the group from all outside enemies as well as for keeping the hostages "in line."

On an individual level, many terrorists suffer from feelings of inadequacy and low self-esteem. This, compounded by the need for security, causes them to band together. Sometimes what the group theoretically stands for is less important. For example, they will *adopt* a cause, not because they truly believe in it, but because the organization associated with the cause will increase their self-esteem and promote a feeling of security.

To illustrate, Moorhead Kennedy remembers one night of his captivity that he spent in the same room with his guards. In the morning, he watched a guard going through the ritual of his Muslim prayers—standing up, kneeling down, and bending over. Then he noticed that the guard was looking at him out of the corner of his eye. "This student," Kennedy told himself, "may really believe in Islam, but he is not really praying. He is going through the motions. These are just the calisthenics of his revolution."

MONEY AND EMPLOYMENT

Terrorists must either support themselves or find sponsors. Some terrorist groups run businesses on the side. One terrorist, for example, had a chicken farm in Iraq before that government threw him out.

Figure 7—Every cause needs money.

Member groups of the Palestine Liberation Organization run businesses. They recruit young people in areas where opportunities are scarce. The young people they hire are also attracted by their nationalist cause. Abu Nidal, as an example, reportedly went to Beirut and recruited young people off the street to carry out the December 1985 attacks at the Rome and Vienna airports. None of his professionals went on those attacks or died in them; only the young recruits, one of whom was a teenager and is now in jail in Italy.

Funding for terrorist groups comes from other sources, too. Some terrorist groups, such as the Palestine Liberation Organization, receive subsidies from governments. Additionally, however, the PLO has extensive investments of its own, in banks and corporations abroad, including some in the United States. Such terrorist groups as the Irish Republican Army receive money from friends abroad. Many of those friends reside in the United States.

Terrorist groups without other bases of financial support often go into various kinds of criminal activity. They rob banks, or, like a Puerto Rican nationalist group in the United States, they hold up armored cars. Groups in Western Europe and South America have kidnapped and held business executives for ransom. They practice extortion, using threats, actual injuries, or damage to property to extract money from victims. Traffic in drugs has been a profitable sideline for many terrorist groups in Latin America and the Middle East. In fact, *narcoterrorism*—defined either as the support of terrorist activity through drug traffic, or the use of terrorism to protect the drug traffic— has become a major element of international terrorism. All of these activities, of course, place the terrorists at the level of criminals.

THE PROFESSIONAL TERRORIST

Becoming a professional terrorist means spending most of the time in hiding, thinking about things like staying alive. If they survive, after years of experience, terrorists can become very skilled at what they do. They have to be, in order to keep themselves or their friends from being caught or killed. In order to hide out "safely," terrorists need help. They often get that help from a government or from other people who expect repayment in some form.

Professional terrorists, like some Palestinian ex

tremists, or like the Turkish gunman reportedly hired by Bulgarians to assassinate Pope John Paul II, often have a state sponsor, and they carry out attacks for their sponsors. Some of them become terrorists for hire. Others split their activities between their own interests and those of their clients. In either case, the professional at some point usually loses any close link back to the original goal or grievance that started him or her on the road to terrorism.

Such professionals and their groups seem to practice terrorism for its own sake. Several groups, such as the Japanese Red Army, Accion Directe in France, the Red Army Faction in Germany, the Lebanese Armed Revolutionary Faction in Europe, and the Italian Red Brigades have developed in this fashion to the point where it is very hard to say what their goals are and specifically how they are trying to reach them.

For these and other reasons, many terrorists, particularly those who have been practicing terrorism for some time, do not welcome peace processes; they oppose solutions to the very grievances that brought them into terrorism in the first place. For the same reason, moderates in their ethnic communities or peacemakers among their own people are often targets of terrorist attacks. Statistics show the most common targets of terrorism by Arabs and other Muslim groups are members of their own peoples.

DEVELOPING MATURE RESPONSES—GROWING UP

Much of terrorist behavior we have looked at, including anger at those from whom they expected too much or attention-getting devices or hitting out at those whom they resent, or who make them feel inferior, are really *immature* behaviors. We have all displayed some of these behaviors when we were younger. Since then, we have tried to develop more grown-up ways to resolve problems; or, realizing that the world will never be exactly as we want it to be, we have learned to live with imperfection.

Similarly, you have learned to live and act responsibly. You may not like the rules you are being asked to follow or some of the institutions we have to live with. Still, you recognize that we often need both. Terrorists, on the other hand, break the rules. They argue that rules, like international law, which governs relations among states, do not apply to them. More than that though, terrorists often break the rules of their own communities; there is no community we know of that considers terrorism to be moral or legal behavior.

Terrorists argue that they have been forced to use behaviors that we call immature and irresponsible because governments and others have not been willing to listen unless terrorist force is used. Sometimes that is only an excuse. But you should ask yourself whether the governments and groups being attacked by terrorists *have* tried to understand terrorist grievances. Have the governments and groups involved made it sufficiently clear that they will respond positively to more mature, less violent approaches? In trying to make such judgments, you should not be guided alone by what the terrorists or their friends say or by what their targets or their friends say. You need to stand back and look at all the evidence before making up your mind.

SUMMARY

Terrorists do what they do for a variety of reasons. Their public motives, or causes, including nationalism, religion, or ethnic and cultural identity are often interrelated. Also instrumental in determining their behavior are feelings like violence, revenge, and fear, and drives for power, money, or professional status. Although much terrorist behavior seems immature, terrorists argue that without such attention-getting devices others will not pay attention to their grievances. Always remain skeptical of what terrorists tell you about their motives since, like the rest of us, they

Figure 8—A terrorist's motives are made up of many different factors.

want to portray their conduct in the most favorable possible light.

REVIEW QUESTIONS

1. Give an example of a terrorist acting through nationalist motives.
2. What is a fanatic?
3. Just because those who belong to other religious or ethnic groups are different from you, does that make them your enemy? Are you their enemy?
4. If a group has strongly held beliefs, do they have the right to use violence to force those beliefs on others?
5. Is terrorism ever used by those who are trying to establish their identity or gain attention for their cause? Give an example. Are there methods, other than terrorism by which they might achieve their goals?
6. Why is revenge not likely to be the only reason Armenian terrorists have killed Turkish diplomats? What other reasons might there be for their actions?

3 | Who Carries Out Terrorist Attacks?

Why has terrorism become more widespread in the past few decades?
Who are the terrorist groups? What are their goals? What are their actions?
Who supports terrorists, or do they act alone?

Is terrorism best described in terms of the people who do it? Or can we describe it better by looking at what terrorists do? We need answers to both these questions. In this chapter and the next one, we will look at some examples from history and at the recent pattern of terrorist activity.

HISTORICAL BACKGROUND

Terror, terrorists, and terrorism have been with us for a long time. History does not tell us when the first attack occurred, who was the first terrorist, or who was the first victim. The risk of being taken hostage and held for ransom while traveling has existed for many centuries. For example, the English people are said to have paid a ransom of 150,000 Austrian marks, which was a very large sum of money in the year 1194, to free King Richard the Lion Hearted, who had been taken hostage while returning from the Third Crusade in the Middle East.

Terrorism is very old in the Middle East. High on the western slope of the Ante-Lebanon Mountains, a ruined castle overlooks the heart of Syria. It once belonged to the Old Man of the Mountain, the leader of the assassins, or *hashishans*. This secret Muslim order murdered many Crusaders while under the influence of hashish, or marijuana, which they culti- vated. In the Biqaa Valley of Lebanon several terrorist groups have recently safehavened under Syrian pro- tection, and now hold Americans hostage. Those groups still grow and sell hashish to support their operations. The link between drugs and terrorism in the Middle East is also a very old one.

From a historical perspective, we can divide terror- ists into two main groups: those who use terror to maintain their power, and those who use terror to seize power. The Reign of Terror during the French Revolution, in the years 1793–94, exemplifies the first group. The radicals or extremists took over the French government from the moderates who had started the revolution. These radicals maintained power by terrorizing those who were against them. Their Revolutionary Courts sentenced opponents to death by drowning or by cutting off their heads with a guillotine.

More recent examples of terrorism by rulers or their agents include:

- the killing, or "liquidation," of rich peasants by Stalin, the ruler of the Soviet Union, in the 1920s;
- the threat, which was never carried out, by Iranian

revolutionaries in 1979–80 to put the American hostages on trial and to execute them;
- the killing of a former Chilean **diplomat** on a street in Washington, D.C. by agents of the present military government of Chile.

Examples of the second group, who use terror to seize power or otherwise to shape events when they are not in power, include:

- political assassins. For example, there was an attempted assassination by an Italian nationalist of the French Emperor Napoleon III. This attempt on his life had the effect of reminding Napoleon III that parts of Italy were still ruled by Austria and of shaming him into war with Austria in 1859 on behalf of Italian unification;
- anarchists who assassinated President McKinley of the United States, as well as some European rulers, in 1901, out of their belief that all rulers and that all governments are evil. They have a modern counterpart in an American group called Posse Comitatus, whose members believe that no government should exist above the level of the county sheriff. Anarchists have been called "ideological terrorists."

As President John F. Kennedy once said, "Terror is not a new weapon. Throughout history, it has been used by those who could not prevail either by persuasion or example." In part, he meant that it is the warfare of people who can't get what they want, no matter how powerful they are. He also suggested, however, that terrorism is a tool of the relatively powerless. For example, the brother of Lenin, the founder of the Soviet Union, was hanged in 1887 for planning to kill Tsar Alexander the Third of Russia. He wrote just before his death: "[Terror] is the only defense to which a minority . . . can resort against the physical strength of the majority."

Terrorism is now a more severe problem for the world community than it has been in the past, for several reasons:

- It is very easy today for terrorists to move from one country to another, to make an attack, and to get away from pursuers.
- Modern weapons are readily available to terrorists and make them much more dangerous and destructive than ever before.
- Terrorism today is very much a **media** event. It is easier for terrorists to publicize their actions and their causes and therefore to cultivate a basis of support.
- Terrorists have developed a network of support arrangements that helps them carry out their attacks and that makes it easier for them to get away.
- In some cases, terrorists in different countries are working together.
- Several modern terrorist groups operate in league with states. Governments of some countries give the terrorists many kinds of help.

WHO ARE THE TERRORISTS?

We have selected the following examples of terrorists groups, of which there are known to be more than one hundred throughout the world, in order to emphasize several important points.

- Terrorist activity is carried out by groups and individuals in many countries—as many as eighty in 1985–86. Most victims of terrorism are people of the same nationality, race, ethnic group, or culture as the terrorists themselves. The United States also has terrorist groups, some which are entirely domestic and some which represent groups in the Middle East, Asia, or elsewhere. You may have thought otherwise because the American media tend to report mainly on incidents that target Americans. The problem is worldwide.

- Terrorist groups differ widely in their makeup, their membership, their motives, goals, and the groups they oppose. At the same time, you will observe some similarities in their weapons, their methods, and the statements used to justify their acts.

Red Army Faction/Baader-Meinhof Gang (RAF). This German ideological terrorist group began its activities in the late 1960's, in the aftermath of West Berlin student demonstrations. The group adopted its name from the Japanese Red Army (a terrorist group that originated in Japan) and got its nickname from the names of two of its leaders, Andreas Baader and Ulrike Meinhof.

Meinhof became the spokesperson for the group. She said that the group's objective was to "hit the Establishment in the face, to mobilize the masses, and to maintain international solidarity." The RAF are really nihilists: They are purely destructive, and they lack positive models for a society to replace the one they want to destroy. They are trying to get the people who are unhappy with their governments to rise up against these governments. They also keep ties with other terrorists groups throughout the world.

The group's biggest terrorist attack was the hijacking in 1977 of a Lufthansa plane with passengers to Mogadishu, the capital of Somalia. A German antiterrorist squad raided the plane and successfully freed the passengers and crew. Since then, the RAF has committed other attacks, such as killing a West German arms manufacturer near his home in 1985.

Popular Front for the Liberation of Palestine (PFLP). This group is led by the notorious George Habash, who was trained as a doctor. They killed twenty-seven innocent travelers and wounded eighty others at Lod (Lydda) International Airport in Israel on May 30, 1972.

The PFLP is one of the almost completely international terrorist organizations. Although its base was originally in Israel, it moved to Jordan, then to Beirut, and now the group conducts its terrorist activities from Aden, South Yemen, and Baghdad, Iraq. It is also supported by Algeria, Libya, and sometimes by the Soviet Union. It also works closely with the Red Army Faction, Carlos the Jackal, the Japanese Red Army, and other groups in Italy, the Netherlands, France, Turkey, and Iran.

Unlike the anarchist Red Army Faction, the PFLP proclaims a nationalist ideology. It desires the complete liberation of the land that was historic Palestine. The PFLP is opposed to any political settlement with Israel, whose right to exist as a state they refuse to recognize. Beyond their nationalistic goal of establishing Palestine as a nation-state, the PFLP supports a Marxist ideology. They consider their enemy to be the whole Western world, including the United States, and the world political and economic system that the West has organized.

Montoneros. This Argentine terrorist organization began as a left-wing group that supported former dictator Juan D. Peron. It has strong connections with the trade union movement in that country. The group made its entrance onto the terrorist scene when it kidnapped and then killed ex-President Pedro Aramburo in May 1970. During the 1970s, it carried out numerous assassinations, bombings, and kidnappings. With the help of the trade unions, it built weapons factories to produce its own arms. Like a number of Latin American terrorist groups, Montoneros received very little outside support for its activities and supported itself through bank robberies and kidnappings. These were ideological terrorists, who claimed to fight against injustice but who appeared to lack a model for a new society to replace the one they fought.

The Order. This American, neo-Nazi, white-**supremacist** ideological terrorist organization was founded in 1983. It ambushed a Brinks security van in 1983 and stole $3.6 million. It also murdered a Jewish radio commentator, Alan Berg, with submachine guns. The group declared that its intention is to make the United States a "white, Christian society." To achieve this model, they think it is necessary to kill Jews, liberals, blacks, federal judges, and government agents.

The Covenant, the Sword, the Arm of the Lord (CSA).
Created in the mid-1970s, this ideological organization believes that God's chosen people do not include such people as Jews and Blacks. The group has been involved in robberies, arsons, bombings, and murder. One CSA member was convicted of the murder of an Arkansas state policeman in 1985.

Prairie Fire Organizing Committee (PFO) / May 19 Communist Organization (M19C). The Prairie Fire Organizing Committee was created in 1974 to serve as a "legal" above-ground, support organization for the Weather Underground Organization, a group which emerged during the 1960s. During that period a number of young people became distrustful of and antagonistic to government and to other institutions of our society. Resistance to the American participation in the Vietnam War, a primary cause of this unrest, is reflected in the Weather Underground's stated dedication to the "overthrow of American **imperialism.**"

Figure 9—In the 1960s some groups brought violence to the nation's capital itself.

The PFO recruited people, provided funding, and distributed propaganda.

In 1976, a split occurred in the Weather Underground. A similar split occurred in the PFO. The offshoot of the PFO, which bases itself on the East Coast, calls itself the May 19 Communist Organization. This terrorist organization has continued to commit crimes, especially in the Washington, D.C. area, where they claimed responsibility for eight bombings between January 1983 and February 1985. Some of these bombings occurred at military facilities, such as Fort McNair and the United States Navy Yard, and at the U.S. Capitol building. We can call these ideological terrorists *nihilistic*, as they have no program of their own other than continued violence and destruction.

Ejército Popular de Boricua (Los Macheteros). This is one of the nationalist terrorist groups in Puerto Rico that wants to liberate the island from the United States. They feel that liberation from the U.S. justifies any acts that are taken to achieve that end, and they call their actions "acts of war."

The Macheteros, who first appeared in 1978, are the most violent terrorists in Puerto Rico. They have bombed the Air National Guard Base, damaging nine planes. They have bombed electrical power stations, conducted armed robberies, and staged attacks against the Federal Building and United States Courthouse in San Juan, Puerto Rico. The latter attacks were accomplished by using a rocket launcher, an example of the sophisticated technology that this terrorist group uses.

WHO HELPS TERRORISTS?

Terrorists need support in order to survive. Their shopping list sounds commonplace: a place to live; a safe home where they will not be detected; food, clothing, medicines, etc. They have to find weapons of one kind or another, depending on the kind of attacks they plan to carry out. They need transportation and ways to communicate with each other or with outsiders. If they travel from one country to another, they need travel documents, including passports and other identification. To obtain all of these things, they need help from people outside their immediate group.

Private Donors

Individuals often provide support. Terrorists very seldom tell people who they are and what they are doing. Therefore, some of the help that terrorists receive is provided by persons who either don't know what the group does or who are deceived into thinking that they are providing help for medical, charitable, or other apparently worthwhile causes.

British sources estimate that private contributions from Americans, mainly those of Irish ancestry, provide the main source of funding for operations of the Irish Republican Army and other Irish nationalist groups in Northern Ireland, most of which practice terrorism. Many people give to a group called Northern Aid, or Noraid, which advertises itself as a charitable organization. The IRA, the PLO, the FMLN in El Salvador, and many other foreign groups operate on a base of voluntary contributions, often from people who do not know they are helping terrorists.

Figure 10—Masked to prevent identification, this squad of the outlawed IRA takes a position behind a barricade during a recent patrol in Londonderry, Northern Ireland. They are reportedly armed with American-made M1 carbines.

Donors are learning, though, that their gift to "charity" might buy guns. Some of them have stopped giving.

State Involvement and Support

Support for terrorist activity is also provided by states. Although state-sponsored terrorism has been around as long as terrorism itself, the problem is now more complex than it was in the past, for several reasons. Today, there are many more nations than before. Half of the nations of the world have been established since World War II. Many of these are anxious to expand their influence, but they lack the **internal political structure,** the military or economic power, or the prestige to pursue their goals as more established states can and do. Some do not want to be identified, at least not publicly, with the goals that they pursue. For both reasons, they often use terrorist groups to carry out their policies.

Some of these nations use their own embassies or *consulates* for terrorist purposes. For example, in 1986 a bomb exploded at a disco in West Berlin, Germany, killing and wounding Americans and others. The Libyan People's Bureau (Libya's name for an embassy) in East Berlin was found to have planned and supported this attack. Not much later, a Palestinian nationalist named Hindawi set up his pregnant Irish girlfriend to carry a bomb on board an Israeli airliner scheduled to leave from London's Heathrow airport. British authorities found that both the Syrian ambassador in London and the Syrian government had been deeply involved in this plot. The British sent the Syrian Ambassador and his staff back to Syria, and closed their embassy in the Syrian capital of Damascus, because of this incident.

Data published by the U.S. Department of State show that three countries—Iran, Syria, and Libya—were involved in close to one hundred terrorist acts in 1985. In that year, the biggest offenders were Syria and Iran, whose agents carried out more than half of the state-supported attacks. However, in 1986 the biggest culprit was Libya, as we can see in the numbers given below.

State-sponsored Terrorist Attacks

	1985	1986
Syria	34	3
Iran	34	8
Libya	14	17
Others	14	2
Total	**96**	**30**

It is not easy to decide what response the United States should make in these cases. All terrorist acts are considered crimes under U.S. law and under the laws of practically all countries. We must ask ourselves, are the terrorism-sponsoring states committing a crime? If they are, should we treat them the way we would treat a criminal at home? How does one get a terrorism-sponsoring state into court? What is the punishment when the state is found guilty? Who carries out the punishment? Later, we will discuss what governments can do about terrorism, state supported and otherwise.

SUMMARY

In our efforts to define terrorism, we have looked at why terrorists do what they do. They have a variety of motivations, including nationalism and ideology. Many are negative in their goals, and destructive. And we have looked more closely in this chapter at who the terrorists are. With roots in the distant past, they are made more dangerous today by better communications, transportation, and equipment. Some are supported by governments, others by private donors. Having looked at specific groups, we can see that terrorists include men and women, young and old, Americans and foreigners. Despite the vast variety of terrorists, one thing ties them together: their violent methods.

REVIEW QUESTIONS

1. Identify a terrorist act from history and one from the last two decades. What are the differences and similarities?
2. Give an example of a terrorist trying to maintain power. Give an example of a terrorist trying to seize power or attention.
3. What are the differences and similarities in the goals, actions, and membership of the RAF, PFLP, and the Monteneros?
4. Are there American terrorist groups? Give some examples.
5. What three countries have been most closely involved in supporting terrorist groups?
6. How might knowing who the terrorists are and who supports them help us respond effectively to terrorism?

4 Recent Patterns

Where do the most terrorist attacks occur?
What are the most common incidents?
Are all terrorist incidents criminal actions?
Who are the most common targets of terrorism?

In the last two chapters, we looked at "why" and "who." In this chapter, we will look closely at the pattern of terrorist activity to get a good sense of the remaining basic issues: "what," "where," and "against whom." Let us now look at some statistics.

WHERE?

Beginning in the early 1980s, international terrorist attacks—those attacks that involve people of more than one country—numbered about 500 each year. By 1986 the number had climbed toward 800 attacks. That averages out to more than two attacks every day.

Terrorist attacks occur on some scale almost everywhere in the world. Figures published each year by the U.S. Department of State in Washington show that most attacks occur in Western Europe, the Mid-

47

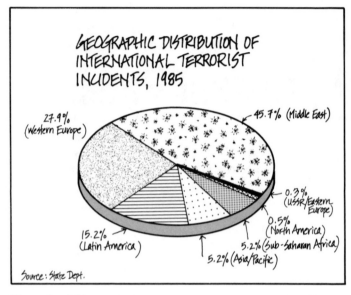

Figure 11—This graph shows that terrorist attacks occur all over the world, although the largest number occur in the Middle East.

dle East, and Latin America. The pattern of attacks is given in State Department figures as shown below:

Terrorist Attacks by World Regions
1981–85

Western Europe	1,103
Middle East	817
Latin America	531
Asia Pacific Region	148
Sub-Sahara Africa	141
North America	81
Soviet Union Eastern Europe	17
Total	**2,838**

Because they must distill a lot of material down to very short reports, the media often do not give us a clear picture of the global pattern of terrorism. We need to look behind the stories to get any real sense of just how widespread a problem terrorism really is.

Attacks do not always happen where the terrorist lives or where the terrorist's problem exists. In the 1980's especially, terrorists have traveled much more, taking their terrorist activity abroad. For this kind of terrorist activity, Western Europe has been the main battleground, and the main source of this terrorism has been the Middle East, as the numbers show us.

Terrorist Attacks of Middle East Origin in Western Europe

1981–85

1981	33
1982	40
1983	33
1984	61
1985	74
Total	**241**

Attacks of Middle East origin have been on the increase. In 1985–86 they accounted for one of every four attacks in Western Europe.

As you might expect, certain countries of Europe have borne the brunt of exported terrorism. There are several reasons for this. Many countries have open borders; they let people come and go freely; they have traditions of very close relations with peoples of Middle Eastern and African origins; and they depend a lot on tourist trade for income.

Middle East Terrorist Attacks in European Countries
1981–85

Austria	10
Cyprus	25
France	35
Greece	37
Italy	32
Spain	21
Turkey	16
United Kingdom	22
West Germany	14

WHO ARE THE VICTIMS?

Since terrorist attacks occur in all regions of the world, anyone can be caught in an attack. No one is free of risk, but diplomats, military personnel, and government officials are common targets. Still, *almost half* of the victims are private citizens, including young people. When terrorists opened fire with machine guns on travelers waiting at Rome International Airport in December 1985, one of the travelers was an eleven-year-old girl named Natasha Simpson. She was traveling with her parents to spend Christmas in the United States. She was shot and killed. As this kind of killing illustrates, no one is really free from the threat of terrorism.

There are great differences among terrorist groups, though, both in how they attack and in the kinds of victims they pick. For example, the group run by Abu Nidal, which has operated out of Iraq, Syria, and Libya, goes in for quick, nasty attacks that hurt people who just happen to be at the scene. Experts believe that this was the group that attacked the Rome and Vienna airports just before Christmas in 1985. Experts say this kind of group does not like long, drawn-out attacks, like hijackings, because their chances of getting caught are too great. These groups also seem to think they get as much publicity as they want for their causes with short, noisy, and damaging attacks.

More often than not, the victims of a hijacking are chosen at random. They just happen to be the people who are on the flight that the hijacker chooses to take over. In our own country, many people have been caught in terrorist situations that way. Maybe you know someone who has had that experience. Perhaps you remember that there were thirty nine Americans held hostage during the takeover of TWA Flight 847. Many people looked at that attack as directed only at Americans. It did not begin that way, because there were many European passengers on board who became bargaining chips in the early phases of the incident. The hijackers let the Europeans off in Algiers before the plane finally landed in Beirut. In Beirut, intense negotiations led to the release of the Americans.

In Western Europe, terrorists groups, such as the Red Army Faction in West Germany or the Red Brigades in Italy, attack mostly government and business targets. In 1985, for example, it is reported that the Red Army Faction members killed a young U.S. soldier to get his identification card, which they used in order to get onto a military base and plant explosives. The resulting bomb blast at Rhein-American Main Air Force base near Frankfort was an attack against the North Atlantic Treaty Organization and the U.S. presence in Germany. Members of Italy's Red Brigades kidnapped former Italian Prime Minister Aldo Moro and kept him for many weeks before killing him. They were trying to threaten or intimidate officials of the Italian government.

The answer to our question, "who gets hurt?" has changed over the years. Early in the 1960s, terrorist groups in such countries as Argentina and Uruguay chose their own government officials and businessmen to be their main targets. Foreigners generally did not get involved. In the late 1960's, foreigners, especially **diplomats,** became the prime targets. During this period, American diplomats were victims in such countries as Brazil, Guatemala, Mexico and the Sudan.

The targeting of diplomats, other government officials, and businessmen continued to dominate terrorist attacks well into the 1980s. However, hijackings, kidnappings, and certain bombings in 1983 and afterward sharply tilted the attacks toward ordinary people. Businessmen and other private citizens came to be the main targets in 1985–86.

In part, this shift reflects the handling of terrorism by the media. As one media person put it, the terrorists provide better entertainment than television script writers can provide, so terrorism gets the media attention. It seems that the terrorists discovered that kidnapping a private citizen made a better story than kidnapping a government official. Media gave the TWA 847 hijacking almost around-the-clock coverage, but practically all of the American victims were just tourists who happened to be in Athens, Greece on the day the hijacking occurred. In a later chapter we will look at the role of media in dealing with a

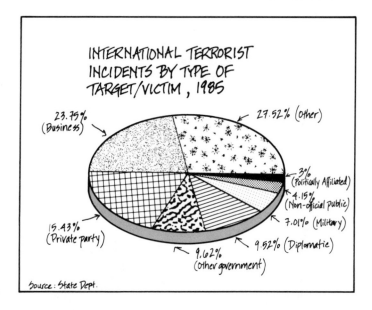

Figure 12—This graph shows the range of people targeted in terrorist attacks.

terrorist incident, but for now remember that terror-ists pick their victims in part for the *publicity* that the victims will bring.

Terrorist attacks have caused death or injury to as many as two thousand people each year since 1983. The chart developed by the State Department on the next page shows this pattern.

Terrorist acts are directed at the people of many different countries. To illustrate, at the beginning of 1987 there were twenty five hostages being held in Lebanon by terrorist groups. These hostages were American, German, French, British, Saudi Arabian, and natives of other Arab countries.

Our newspapers, magazines, radio, and television spend a lot of time talking about terrorist attacks

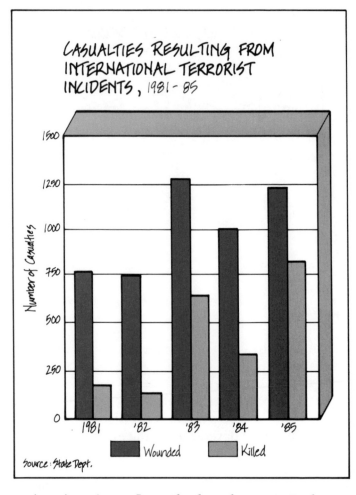

CASUALTIES RESULTING FROM INTERNATIONAL TERRORIST INCIDENTS, 1981-85

Source: State Dept.

against Americans. In truth, though, most attacks are carried out against people of other countries. In 1985, for example, only twenty two percent of the incidents involved attacks against Americans. Israel had more casualties than we did in that year, but the largest group of casualties were Western Europeans.

Americans have been the subjects of international terrorist attacks in many different places. In the 1980s, Chile, Colombia, France, Italy, Lebanon, Namibia, and the Philippines are but a few of the places where Americans have been harmed or kidnapped.

WHAT?

Terrorists mostly use bombings, **arson,** and kidnappings as their means of attack. Although kidnappings receive much of the media attention, more than half of the attacks are bombings. The State Department figures for 1981–85 show the following pattern:

Kinds of International Terrorist Attacks Against U.S. Citizens and Property

1981–85

Armed attacks	99
Arson	154
Bombings	436
Hostage situations	7
Kidnappings	60
Hijackings	2
Skyjackings	18
Other	87
Total	**863**

As you see, there have not been very many hijackings of ships. One of the two shown was the piracy of the Italian cruise ship *Achille Lauro* in 1985 by members of the Palestine Liberation Front, a splinter group of the Palestine Liberation Organization, the PLO.

As we showed in the table above, the most common types of attacks are bombings, armed attacks, arson, hijackings,and hostage-takings. To better understand the nature of these attacks, we will look at a number of specific cases. As you look at these cases, think about the problem of definition and try to decide whether the acts were terrorist in nature or something else. Each of the incidents outlined below occurred in 1985.

Japan. The radical group Chukaku-ha said it launched homemade rockets at the U.S. Consu-

Figure 14—This photo shows the body of one of the four marines killed in El Salvador in a June 1985 terrorist incident. The body is being carried onto a C-141 Starlifter aircraft for return to Andrews Air Force Base, Maryland.

late in Kobe. No one was hurt, and the building was not damaged.

Portugal. A group called "Popular Forces of 25 April" carried out a mortar attack against warships anchored in Lisbon Harbor. The ships flew the national flags of countries of the North Atlantic Treaty Organization

West Germany. Two members of the group called the Red Army Faction entered the home of industrialist Ernst Zimmerman.They tied him to a chair and shot him.

Greece. Members of the group called "17 November" shot a Greek publisher on the street in Athens and critically wounded his driver.

Canada. Three members of an Armenian group called the Armenian Revolutionary Army seized the Turkish Embassy. They killed a guard. The Turkish ambassador escaped by jumping out a window.

Lebanon. Gunmen abducted Associated Press correspondent Terry Anderson. They have now held him captive for two years.

Italy. Members of Italy's Red Brigades assassinated a well-known Rome University professor, Enzio Tarantelli. Professor Tarantelli worked with Italian labor organizations.

Spain. People who claimed to represent several groups bombed a restaurant outside Madrid, killing eighteen people and wounding eighty two others, including fifteen Americans.

Sri Lanka. Members of a Tamil separatist group carried out a machine gun attack at the ruin of the historic city of Anaradhapura. The victims were men, women, children, and Buddhist monks and nuns.

El Salvador. Members of a group called the Pedro Pablo Castillo Front claimed responsibility for kidnapping President Napoleon Duarte's daughter, Inez. They kept her prisoner for two months and traded her for the release of two dozen **guerrillas** being held by the government of El Salvador.

The United States. During November 1985 a U.S. Army Major was ambushed and killed in the Puerto Rican city of San Juan. The Puerto Rican nationalist group called the Macheteros said that it carried out this attack.

SOME ISSUES OF DEFINITION

Terrorism vs. Crime

As you look at the cases with the background you now have, you can often guess the reasons why a terrorist group is doing something by studying the kind of attack a group uses. However, there will be cases that puzzle you because the goal of the terrorists will not be clear. Robbing a bank, for example, looks like an ordinary crime. How does the terrorist justify it as a political act? Shooting a businessman or a government official on the street may be an act of revenge or an act designed to intimidate others. In Northern Ireland members of the IRA shot jurors who were hearing cases against accused terrorists to persuade other jurors not to bring in guilty verdicts. Members of Italy's Red Brigades used the same tactics on businessmen to intimidate them, in some cases to persuade other businessmen to pay ransoms.

Some of the attacks just listed look like ordinary crime, and some of them look like warfare. The official statistics of our own government and of the other governments involved usually treat all these cases as terrorism. Are they all acts of terrorism in your judgment? Which ones do you think are not? Why? The line between an ordinary crime and a terrorist crime is often difficult to draw. How terrorism is defined by law helps give a more thorough understanding of the acts.

The laws of our country and of most countries of the world treat terrorist acts as criminal acts. Under U.S. federal, state, and local laws, any act of terrorism is dealt with as a crime. These acts are covered under headings that are very familiar to you: murder, robbery, kidnapping, arson, hijacking, skyjacking, extortion, destruction of property, and other crimes.

The legal treatment of terrorism reveals an important distinction: If an act of terrorism occurs entirely within our own country, the acts are treated as criminal acts and we can handle them through normal law enforcement procedures. If a terrorist attacks someone here, the police investigate. When the terrorist is apprehended, he or she will be put in jail, given a fair trial, and if found guilty, sent to prison.

Other governments define and deal with terrorism at home in this same way, but the international cases pose a special problem because more than one government gets involved. In some cases, several governments have to get involved to protect their citizens, their territory, or other interests. We will come back to this area of dealing with terrorism when we talk

about what other governments are doing and what
our own government can do.

SUMMARY

The number of terrorist attacks has increased dramatically in recent years, rising to more than two incidents each day. The largest number of attacks occur
in Western Europe and in the Middle East. Terrorist
actions, like bombings, murder, and arson, reveal
that terrorists commit acts that are crimes under the
codes of law of most countries. When a terrorist
incident involves more than one country, the country
where the attack occurred often handles the incident.
But each situation can often be quite complex. Finally, a look at specific cases shows that anyone,
whether an ordinary civilian or a diplomat or military
official, can be a victim of a terrorist act.

REVIEW QUESTIONS

1. Is any region of the world free of terrorist attacks?
2. Where are the largest number of attacks?
3. Is any person free from the danger of terrorist
   attack?
4. Who are the most common targets?
5. How many people were killed or injured by terrorist attacks in 1985?
6. What are the most common methods of terrorist
   attack?
7. What are the differences and similarities between
   terrorism and crime?

5 Contemporary Issues

What is the role of the media regarding terrorism?
Should we negotiate with terrorists?
Do terrorists succeed?
How can governments respond to terrorism?

THE MEDIA AND TERRORISM

Although publicizing a cause is not the only objective of terrorist activity, it is an important one. The hostages in Tehran were told by their guards: "You don't realize it, but we're on prime time."

In Northern Ireland, the Irish Republican Army has tried for years to make itself look like a regular army fighting in a civil war. Both British and Irish authorities consider the IRA nothing more than a terrorist group. In order to look legitimate before the public, the IRA holds large military funerals with flags, pipe bands, military honors, and weapons, when one of their members is killed. They invite television crews to cover these funerals so that viewers will come away with the impression that the IRA is a regular army.

Many people argue that the television networks should not be allowed to cover such events, since

Figure 15—Should there be limits placed on the media's coverage of terrorist incidents?

they are giving publicity to terrorists and thus promoting their causes. In reply, the networks argue that terrorist incidents are news. Let the viewers, they say, make up their *own* minds about what is going on.

Suppose you side with those who want to cut down on the showing of terrorist events in the media. People would argue against you by saying that the U.S. Constitution, in its First Amendment, guarantees *freedom of the press.* The Supreme Court has ruled that criminals, even after being convicted, are entitled to their First Amendment rights. They can write books or give statements to the press and television, which media can use or not. This means that terrorists in democratic societies are protected by the same rights. Many people would argue that freedom of the press is a vital guarantee of other liberties. Perhaps, to protect the freedom itself, we may have no choice but to allow terrorists to **publicize** their causes. Protecting First Amendment rights may mean that the public should not be prevented from learning what the terrorists have to say, whether or not it is legitimate.

Some people who oppose media coverage of terrorist events argue that if the terrorists are denied the chance to gain the publicity they seek, they might not commit so many terrorist acts. We have seen, however, that terrorists have a variety of motives for what they do. Publicity is only one factor.

To understand the complexity of the media issue, consider the following example: Assume a case where the terrorist is primarily seeking publicity. Assume that either by government regulation or the media's own guidelines, terrorist events cannot le-

Figure 16—This photo shows a cameraman a few feet from an armed policeman taking his position when Hanafi Muslims took over three Washington, D.C. buildings in 1977.

gally be publicized. Then, consider a real situation: You may have heard of the case of the man in a van full of dynamite who threatened to blow up the Washington Monument. That incident received wide media publicity. Could an event of such magnitude be kept off TV? If so, the public would be denied a serious news event. Furthermore, if terrorist incidents are kept off TV, terrorists may just create more serious incidents, possibly with even greater casualties.

On the other hand, what the media does with a terrorism story can lead to grave results. For example, David Jacobsen, a former hostage in Lebanon, was once prompted by his terrorist captors to make a videotape to be shown on American TV. After the tape was shown, a TV commentator wondered aloud on camera whether or not Jacobsen might not have been sending coded messages. A tape of this broadcast was seen by Jacobsen's captors. They accused him of being a spy and beat him badly.

You might well decide that the media ought to solve this problem themselves. The media can decide for themselves, for example, that they are not going to report things during a terrorist incident that will get people hurt or killed. They can decide not to report things that might cause terrorists to keep captives longer or to take other captives. They can decide for themselves not to report a terrorists incident live, which is a situation in which the terrorists, not the media, control the story. They can decide not to try themselves to negotiate with terrorists or to act in a role that would be appropriate only for government. The media can also decide to stay out of issues that might be central and sensitive in a negotiation between a government and the terrorists. Most important, though, and especially related to the First Amendment, is the question of who makes these decisions. Some people have talked about establishing government guidelines, but under the Constitution, it is the media's call.

In all this discussion, the key words, for both government and media, are responsibility, self-discipline, and good judgment. In the media, the overall decisions on what will be presented and how it will be presented are made by editors who exercise what is called **editorial judgment.** Each terrorist episode will require the weighing of all the factors that we have been discussing.

In summary, terrorists use the media to publicize their causes. Many people therefore argue that TV networks should not report or give time to terrorist events. Others argue in reply that the First Amendment guarantee of freedom of the press is a more important consideration. In a democracy, the argument says, the public should be allowed to make up its own mind, based on all available information, including what the terrorists have to say. Sometimes media coverage can endanger sensitive negotiations in progress, or the safety and welfare of hostages. The key word is judgment, and today, that judgment is made by the media.

NEGOTIATIONS WITH TERRORISTS

The United States has a stated policy of "no concessions to terrorists." Some people, even government officials, have interpreted that policy to mean no negotiations and no dialogue with terrorists. But we *deal* with terrorists whenever we must, and negotiating at some level is an unavoidable part of dealing with them.

Negotiation is an important word, not just in connection with terrorism, but because we **negotiate** more often than we realize. Imagine the following example: When you were younger and you agreed to do the dishes *if* your mother let you stay up late to watch TV, you were negotiating. You would also negotiate if you were buying a used car. The salesman would name a price. You would offer less. Then the two of you would probably settle on a price that was somewhere in between the two figures.

In the example, the negotiation with your mother involves much more than a TV program. You probably live in the same house and see and talk with her everyday. In the second case, whether or not you buy the car you probably will never see the salesman again. You can walk away from the negotiation if you feel the price he quotes is still too high. With the salesman, you are negotiating "at arms length," and that determines the way you negotiate and how tough you are prepared to be.

Now look at a case where a lone hostage-taker is holding a small boy and demanding an airline ticket out of the country. This case actually happened in Texas in early 1987. How is the bargaining different? Part of what has happened is that the hostage-taker has forced you into making some kind of a deal against your will, and maybe against your interests. We call that "negotiating under **duress.**"

Terrorism gets people into that kind of dilemma. Moorhead Kennedy remembers the question of negotiation as it applied to the hostage crisis in Iran:

About 10 days after we had been taken hostage, we asked a guard, "When will we be going home?" The guard replied, that they hoped it would be soon. Then he added, "We want the Shah."

There was no way, I thought to myself, that the U.S. government would be blackmailed into sending the Shah back from the United States to Iran to face trial and certain execution. I remembered when I used to argue that the United States should never pay ransom for hostages. It should not even _talk_ to terrorists. That way, the terrorists would learn that there was no advantage to taking people hostage. But now, in Tehran, there I was, possibly to be shot if the U.S. did not hand back the Shah.

After a while, I learned that wanting the Shah was not the real reason they were holding us hostage. Basically the students took over the Embassy in order to keep the Iranian people excited about their revolution, until the students could get their radical friends into power. When that was done, the Ayatollah Khomeini, who used this student movement to strengthen his power, agreed to our release.

In every negotiation, there are three questions to be answered: What do the parties _say_ they want? What do they _really_ want? What are they willing to _settle for_? Let us examine this case, to see how these questions apply.

In analyzing this bargaining situation, notice its similarity to dealing with the used car salesman. Remember what he _said_ he wanted: the high price that you were not willing to pay. What the salesman really wanted, however, was to sell the car at some profit. You wanted to buy a car as cheaply as possible.

All you had to negotiate was the price. Probably the salesman got less than he hoped for, and you paid a little more. You both were willing to settle on that basis.

The Iranians had their objective. Although they said they wanted the Shah, what they really wanted was to use the hostages to help move their revolution in the direction and at the speed they wanted. The U.S. government, on the other hand, wanted to get the hostages back under circumstances that would not lessen the dignity of the United States or that would make future hostage-holding look profitable.

For many months, there appeared to be no way the two sets of objectives could be brought together or a settlement could be reached. Then, in September 1980, the Iranian Revolutionary Parliament met for the first time and gave Khomeini the power position he wanted. There was no longer any reason to keep the hostages. In the meantime, Iran and Iraq had gone to war and the Iranians needed money to pay for the war. They were ready to bargain.

The U.S. Government held Iranian monies. On that basis, a settlement became possible. The negotiations took a long time, from September 1980 to January 1981, because the U.S. government demanded some of the Iranian monies it was holding to be set aside to pay off the claims of American banks and businesses against Iran. Finally, the Iranians agreed, the U.S. released the monies, and the hostages came home.

How you negotiate with terrorists and what you negotiate about depends on the circumstances of the individual case. There are, however, some general rules:

1. It is important during a terrorist incident to establish and keep up a dialogue with terrorists. For example, the State Department very often maintains an open telephone line to the location of a terrorist incident in progress. Thus during a hijacking of an Air France flight by alleged Palestinians in 1983, Terry Arnold had this talk on the telephone with a contact where the plane was on the ground in Catania, Sicily, surrounded by Italian security guards:

    CONTACT: "Terry, the hijackers want fuel so they can take off. What do you think?"

Figure 17—Establishing and maintaining a dialogue with terrorists can be an important part of dealing with a terrorist situation. Here, the phone line used by the Hanafi Muslim terrorists in the Washington, D.C. incident.

TERRY: "I'd rather keep them on the ground; it's a lot safer for passengers, the crew, and the plane. What do the Italian authorities think? It's their decision."

CONTACT: "Just a minute." (Some delay) "The Italian officer in charge says they—the terrorists—want to trade passengers for fuel."

TERRY: "A lot of passengers?"

CONTACT: "He doesn't know. Maybe thirty five or forty, he says."

TERRY: "That sounds like we could cut way down on the number of people in danger. Does the Embassy have any problem?"

CONTACT: "No. Unless you all disagree we are not going to pose any objection to letting them refuel and take off on this basis."

As you see in this example, by talking as the Italian officials did with the terrorists, you smoke out what the terrorists really want, and what they might be willing to settle for. Sometimes that can be very helpful in ending an incident or in getting people out safely. Also, when a plane has been hijacked, and passengers' lives are threatened by jumpy and trigger-happy terrorists, you *keep* talking. That is one way to calm terrorists down.

2. Respond to "routine" demands—if they want food, water, or fuel, give it to them. What you are doing in such a case is buying time. Routine demands must be met, in any case, unless you are prepared to starve and dehydrate the victims along with the terrorists. Hostages need food,

drink, sleep, air, exercise, toilets. The necessities of life must be provided, in order for negotiations to continue.

3. Show your strength. It may look like the terrorists have the upper hand. Remember, however, that they want something that you have very badly. That usually evens out the negotiation. Your immediate need, while you figure out how to work the problem, is to deter them from injuring or killing the hostages. President Carter sent messages to the Iranian students, saying that *if* the hostages were injured, put on trial, or executed, he would launch a military strike against Iran. His warnings—his show of strength—may have saved the hostages' lives.

4. Be patient. Usually, time is on your side. Let the hostage-holders tire themselves out. They will be easier to deal with.

5. Avoid discussions of demands you don't want to meet. For example, avoid:

   A. **Concessions** that run counter to the honor and dignity of a nation or are contrary to what you believe to be right. In the Iran hostage case, returning the Shah to be executed was one such demand. An apology by the United States for its past policies in Iran was another. That would have diminished the dignity of the U.S. in the eyes of the world.

   B. Concessions which might give an excuse for, or encouragement to, other terrorist acts. For example, the Shiites who are holding many hostages in Lebanon have offered to release them if the United States, Germany, Britain, and others pressure the government of Kuwait to release from jail against seventeen terrorists convicted of bombing the French and American Embassies and four other targets in that country. If the governments had agreed to the demand, then every terrorists would understand that in order to spring other terrorists from jail they need only kidnap more hostages.

6. Negotiate with terrorists to win, if you can. That means getting hostages back safely without making unacceptable concessions.

In summary, negotiating with terrorists, like any other negotiation, involves three questions: What do the parties say they want, what do they *really* want, and what are they willing to settle for? Where lives of hostages are at stake, keep talking, if only to calm the terrorists down. By talking, you may also smoke out what they really want. Respond to routine demands, like food and water for hostages. Avoid discussing demands that you don't want to meet, especially those which, if agreed to, would encourage terrorists to take more hostages. Patience is critical. Your goal is to bring hostages home safely, but without making unacceptable concessions to terrorist demands.

DO THE TERRORISTS SUCCEED?

Faced with all of the publicity about terrorist attacks, it is often hard to tell who is coming out on top. What kinds of things do you look at to decide whether the terrorists are getting what they want? You need to look at the short-term and the long-term terrorist situation:

> —**In the short run:** 1) Are the terrorists able to pull off their attacks successfully? 2) Are they frightening and hurting people? 3) Are they getting attention? 4) Are they getting away with their attacks, or 5) are they getting caught?

You can answer the first three questions with a yes. The answers to the fourth and fifth questions are that often they get away, but many of them get caught— if not right away, then in due course. Many members of the German Red Army Faction are in prison. So are many members of the Italian Red Brigades. In early 1987, French authorities found and arrested the four key members of the group Accion Directe. Terrorist groups in the United States have not fared well, either. The leadership of the United Freedom Front and The Order are in prison, and several members of other groups are in prison or under indictment. Others may remain free, but always in hiding.

Some terrorist groups, like many of those in the Middle East, have the sponsorship and protection of a government. Syria lets several groups, including those holding American hostages, live and work in Syrian-controlled areas in Lebanon. Libya provides a **safehaven** and training for different groups. Maybe such groups do not have to hide from their sponsors, but they are careful not to be found or seen by outsiders.

> —**In the long run:** 1) Are the terrorists achieving their political goals? 2) Are they making headway

on issues that matter? 3) If not, are they creating an environment for future success?

The answers to these three questions are: (1) not very often, (2) not very well, and (3) not in very many places. The short-run mayhem and publicity do not deliver much long-term political success. However, there have been some successes. For example, the Stern and Irgun groups in Palestine were instrumental in gaining independence and political recognition for the new state of Israel in 1948. Israel became a democracy. Kenya gained its independence in part through the terrorist activities of the Mau Mau. As another example, with considerable help from the United States the Sandinistas were able to overthrow their former dictator, Anastasio Somoza, and take over Nicaragua. But Nicaragua is now a dictatorship under the Sandinistas. On the other hand, as you can see in the media every day, the warring ethnic and religious factions in Lebanon are killing one another and using terrorism against each other without visible gains. In Argentina more than a decade ago, the Montoneros tried to take over the country by using urban terrorism. In the end many of the Montoneros were killed or imprisoned. Others simply disappeared. On the other side of the River Plate, the Tupamaros of Uruguay almost succeeded in destroying their country, while most members of their group were killed and the group itself was disbanded. The record for the long run, therefore, is that sometimes terrorism works, but more often it doesn't.

How Successful Has Terrorism Been in Affecting Our Lives?

One further question is, what is terrorism doing to the rest of us? Terrorism clearly is affecting us. It is changing the way we travel and the things we have to do when we travel. Terrorism is limiting our choice of destination. It is changing the way we think about some regions of the world. Does that mean that the terrorists are succeeding in what they set out to accomplish? Probably not. Many people, as we discussed earlier, have changed their travel plans, but that does not mean they have changed their views on issues in the Middle East, in Central America, or in Europe, where most terrorist attacks occur. Here the question is not whether the terrorists are *bothering us*, it is really whether they are *persuading us* that what they want makes sense. Do you think the pattern of attacks in the Middle East in 1985–86 helped the cause of the Palestinian people? Many people think the attacks on TWA Flight 847 and on the *Achille Lauro* ended up hurting terrorist interests.

GOVERNMENTS' RESPONSES TO TERRORISM

As we begin to study what governments are doing about terrorism, we need to ask: Where do most terrorist actions occur? Because most incidents occur well outside American territory, these actions are legally outside our jurisdiction. It is not easy for the U.S. to assert authority, express preferences, or impose wishes on some other government or people. International terrorism often involves several different governments.

Given those limits on freedom of action, suppose you are a head of state or a member of a country's legislature. Your task is to make policy to deal with international terrorism. What are the most important things you would try to do? Keep in mind that there are two broad classes of things you can do about terrorism. One class consists of things you can do right now, and they will have some impact right now. The other class of actions you can start right now, but you should not expect any results for a longer time.

Let's look first at the things governments could do right now. Here is a short list for our discussion:

- Improve the security at places that terrorists usually attack.
- Teach people who are at risk what they can do to protect themselves.
- Get other governments to do something about public safety in their countries.
- Improve public safety conditions in your own country.
- Improve police work and background checks on terrorist groups and terrorist activities.
- Gather more accurate **intelligence** about what terrorists are doing.
- Learn all you can about the technology of terrorism.
- Take a closer look at travelers who cross your borders.
- Pay close attention to groups in your country who have a history of terrorism.

Many governments are doing something in all of the areas that we have just outlined. Each country's situation, however, is a little different. Countries have

Figure 18—This marine, armed with an M-47 Dragon antitank weapon, stands guard near a marine battalion headquarters and barracks in Beirut, Lebanon. The photo was taken in November 1983.

different laws, and they face different terrorist threats. They react to the threat of terrorism somewhat differently. Although each country's situation is different, reactions to the threat of terrorism are quite similar.

The following scenario shows what actions governments have taken in recent years because of the rise of terrorism: If you were to go on a trip to Europe, you would see the many different steps different countries are using to guard their citizens and tourists against the terrorist threat. On the day you arrive at the airport, the airline looks at your tickets and looks at your passport to see that your travel documents are in order for arrival in a foreign country, and then you have your first meeting with the impact of terrorism. There in front of you stands a security guard looking you over and asking you to put your luggage on a conveyer belt. The conveyer belt takes your luggage and X-rays it to see if there is anything dangerous in it. In the meantime, you walk through a metal detector to see if you are carrying any dangerous instruments. As you move through the waiting room and onto the airplane, you notice that only people who have some specific task to carry out to prepare for your flight are allowed anywhere near the airplane. All of these security precautions are in reaction to the threat of terrorism.

Your overnight flight to London is uneventful, and you arrive very early in the morning at London's Heathrow Airport. One of the first things that strikes you is that there are security guards everywhere. Corridors are blocked, passageways are restricted, and security guards control access to most areas. The guards carry submachine guns. You have had your second introduction to the effects of terrorism. As you go through passport control (everyone flying in from another country must go through this checkpoint), you discover that the officer studies your passport carefully. He glances down at the top of his desk where, although you can't see it, he has a list of possible terrorist suspects. He looks at your name to see if it's on the list. Finally, you are clear of all the formalities and you are on your way to London.

Your hotel is around the corner from the famous Grosvenor Square. As you approach your hotel you pass by the American Embassy, which dominates one end of the square. Out front you notice a policeman standing and observing people. Across the street you see a black vehicle with people in uniform motionless inside. As you look at the embassy, you notice that doors and windows look secure. Windows on the lower floors appear to be made of very heavy glass. They are. Windows on the upper floors have curtains wadded up in a strange fashion down at the bottom almost as if they were never hemmed up and finished. Those are blast curtains designed to absorb some of the effects if a bomb explodes outside.

As you arrive at your hotel, you have not really begun your European vacation yet, but you've already had four encounters with the effects of terrorism. Remember what they were because every time you take off in an airplane, you will go through the procedure you just went through. Every time you get off, you will see the systems that you saw on arrival in London. Every time you approach an embassy, not only an American embassy, you will see some version of the security that you saw around Grosvenor Square.

Western European governments are looking with increasing care at people who come to visit their countries. You will remember from our statistics that one out of every four terrorist attacks in Western Europe was carried out by terrorists from the Middle East in 1985 and 1986. In early 1987, you may recall German authorities captured one of the TWA flight 847 hijackers as he tried to enter Germany at Frankfurt. He was carrying liquid explosives. Apparently, he planned to use them to carry out terrorist attacks in Germany. We talked earlier about the bomb attacks in France that were carried out by a group called the Lebanese Armed Revolutionary Faction in order to

Figure 19—To respond to the danger of terrorism, Americans overseas must often operate under tight security.

get one of its leaders out of jail. Such incidents have caused European governments to be much more careful about the people they allow to enter their countries. One of the signs of that, you will discover, is that when you arrive in Paris you have to have a visa in your passport to enter France. That is a new rule, a rule the French adopted very reluctantly because they have always had very open borders. But the movement of terrorists forced this decision on them.

European governments, as well as the U.S. government, have also had to look more closely at foreigners who are **residents** in their countries. These resident aliens are people who are either in exile or residents who are employed in some capacity. The reason for the closer look is that governments have encountered a number of such residents who are involved in terrorism. Shortly after the arrest of the TWA Flight 847 hijacker in Frankfurt, German authorities found that his brother was living in Germany. When they raided his house, they discovered weapons probably intended to support terrorist activity in Europe.

Special Forces

Most governments of Western Europe have had to create special forces to respond to terrorist attacks. The British have created the so-called Special Air Service Regiment (SAS). Germany has formed the force called Grenzschutzgruppe (GSG-9). France, Italy, and other countries of the area have such forces as well. The United States maintains a special force called Delta for this purpose.

To support response groups like those, it is necessary to have very good information. Governments in Western Europe have been cooperating more actively on information about who comes in and who goes out of their country. These governments are developing some common technologies that could be helpful in responding to terrorism. They have also begun to train their public officials and law enforcement officers to do a better job both at anticipating and responding to terrorist attacks.

Long-run Actions

Now let's look for a moment at the long-term approach in combatting terrorism. It starts with training people to cope with and to manage many different aspects of the problem of international terrorism. To get good intelligence, for example, there is a need for new intelligence officers who are well trained in the street-level police work that is involved in dealing with terrorism. To anticipate terrorist attacks and plan ahead to meet them, people who are well trained in such diverse subjects as weaponry, combat tactics, psychology, and, of course, the history of terrorist activity in their country are needed.

But the hardest part of the long-term attack on terrorism is deciding what to do about the underlying causes of terrorism. In the short run, you can find the terrorists, try them, convict them, and put them in jail. But that only deals with the terrorist's immediate act. It does not deal with the problems that generated terrorist action in the first place.

At the very beginning of our study, you will remember, we said that one of the questions you should think about is what can be done about the grievances of the terrorist. Can we find nonviolent means to deal with these grievances? Is the grievance the kind of thing that cannot be fixed in any reasonable way? If the cause of the terrorist grievance can be removed, how do we remove it? Does the answer lie with improved economic conditions? Does one answer lie in dealing with the aspirations of such people as the Palestinians, craving for a homeland? Can we deal with some of the problems by having more universally accepted principles respecting the protection of human rights? Are there other aspects of the long-term problem that we can deal with through international agreements and treaties between countries?

As you can see readily from this list of questions, you must look carefully at each case when trying to evaluate terrorist grievances. There is simply no way you can make good, blanket decisions. Yet, it is essential to find answers that fit a large number of cases, while protecting your own institutions and values.

In dealing with any aspect of international terrorism, cooperation with other governments is essential The U.S. has agreed to a series of international obli-

Figure 20—International law is one way governments from different countries can cooperate on the problem of terrorism.

gations respecting the handling of cases that might arise in areas such as hostage-taking, hijacking, the protection of diplomats, and so on. Recent terrorist attacks have underscored the need for cooperation with other governments in several areas. Unfortunately, one result is that travelers lose the ease with which they have been able to move across another country's borders in the past. Increased border control and the difficulty involved in obtaining the documents needed to enter a country reflect part of the price we pay to control terrorism.

What Can the United States Do?

What can the United States do about terrorism? Let's split the discussion of what the United States can do into two parts. The first part deals with what can the United States do alone to cope with the problem; the second part deals with what it can do with the help of other countries.

Acting on its own, the United States can do the following:

- Improve the physical security of our embassies, military bases, and other overseas facilities;

- Train our people to provide better security for themselves and for others—in great part, this means
  learning to apply the kind of rules we have outlined
  for you;
- Provide security for people who visit the United
  States;
- Establish effective laws to deter terrorist acts and to
  deal with terrorism when it occurs;
- Be sure that we try in our own country to deal fairly
  and promptly with people's legitimate grievances;
- Be prepared to help other countries deal with their
  terrorist problems; and
- When other methods fail be prepared to use the
  police or military force to deal with a terrorist situation.

These are the basic strategies that our government
applies now. Keep in mind that all levels of government are involved. Under federal law, the FBI is
involved in any terrorist incident inside the U.S., but
heavy responsibilities fall on state and local authorities to manage individual incidents. This includes
negotiating with terrorists or others in hostage situations; maintaining so-called SWAT teams (special
weapons and tactics teams)for use in emergencies;
and working with the community to deal with people's grievances.

As you can see, we can do a lot for ourselves. But
the things we do with other governments remain the
most important. Practically every international terrorist incident involving the citizens or the property of
the United States has occurred in a foreign country.
In recent years those incidents increasingly have occurred in Western Europe. Every international inci-

dent by definition involves at least two countries. Thus, even though there are many things we must do for ourselves, most of the things we must do will require some cooperation from other countries.

Therefore, all the things other governments are doing about terrorism are of great interest to the United States. The first thing the United States must do is to find ways to work with other governments to combat terrorism.

What About the Use of Force?

Every time there is a major terrorist incident somewhere, the question comes up, "Should the United States use force to stop the terrorists?" That's a good question, and the answer is not just one-sided. The United States, like all countries of the world, has a right to defend its people, its property, and its territory from attack. This includes attacks by terrorists or by anyone else who may threaten our country in any way. The right of self-defense was included in the United Nations Charter as Article 51. There are four basic questions that need to be answered in deciding whether to use force:

1. Are there options other than force that will help you get your people back safely and promptly?
2. Can you use force without harm to innocent bystanders?
3. Will your use of force be supported or opposed by other governments?
4. Is it likely that your use of force will be successful?

A country faced with a critical terrorist situation needs to answer these questions. If they cannot be answered satisfactorily, it seems wiser not to use force. It is necessary, however, to keep the force option available because it can often speed up negotiations and deter additional terrorist actions.

When any government talks about using force to deal with terrorism, other governments experience a nagging concern about the possible invasion or intrusion into their territory. We would be concerned too, if we thought some other country might send in troops to rescue its embassy staff here from a terrorist takeover. Such a possibility is scary, to say the least.

An issue like the possible use of force pushes governments to cooperate with one another, both to deal with terrorism and to avoid harm to their diplomatic relations. Ask yourself how you would handle this kind of a decision. If another government wanted to use force within your boundaries, what questions would you ask? Would it make a difference to you if some of your own people were hostages? What if several governments were involved because their people were also hostages in the incident?

Many factors need to be considered as we try to deal with modern terrorism. Handling any terrorist situation effectively requires several responses from us. We must pay close attention to the handling of media coverage during a terrorist event. We must also work to uncover the real motives of the terrorist group. Once the motives and demands are understood, negotiation can take place. Finally, we need to work cooperatively with other countries to tighten security and to provide mutual protection from terrorist acts.

REVIEW QUESTIONS

1. Should there be restrictions on the media's coverage of terrorism? Who would decide what these restrictions would be?
2. If you were secretary of state and you knew that a senior reporter at a national newspaper had information on secret negotiations with a terrorist group involving American hostages, under what circumstances, if any, would you ask the reporter not to print the story?
3. What is an example of the media's coverage of a terrorist incident directly resulting in harm to a hostage?
4. What are the pluses and minuses of negotiating with terrorists? Of not negotiating with terrorists?
5. What are some of the guidelines for dealing with terrorism?
6. Do terrorists succeed in the short term? In the long term?
7. Has terrorism affected anyone you know? How?
8. How can governments cooperate to combat terrorism?
9. Should force always be an option in dealing with terrorism? What are the advantages and disadvantages of considering force?

6 | **What Can You Do?**

How can you avoid a terrorist incident?
How do you deal with a terrorist incident if you yourself are in one?
What are some of the lessons of terrorism?

In the previous chapter we considered the questions: "Are terrorists winning?" and "What responses are there to terrorist activity?" In this chapter we will talk about some rules you yourself can follow in dealing with terrorism and terrorists. Then we will look at the things you can do and ways you can think that will help you avoid terrorist attacks. Toward the end of this chapter we will consider things you might do in the event that you do get caught in a terrorist attack. We consider the chances of that ever happening to be very slim, but we think it is worthwhile to think about how to deal with that kind of a crisis.

DEALING WITH TERRORISM

Keeping Yourself and Others out of Trouble

The first rule for dealing with terrorism yourself is the same as a basic rule for playing any sport: Don't let the other side get you **psyched out**. If you are going into a region or a situation where the risk of a terrorist attack is high, keep cool, think, and pay attention to what is happening around you.

With that opening piece of advice, let's back off and look the situation over a bit. How much of this problem can you manage yourself? Let's look at the day-in-day-out things you control. When you are not at home, at work, or in school, you decide where you are going to go, how you will get there, who you will go with, who you will see, what you will do when you get there, how long you will stay, how you will get home. If you did those things the same way all the time and in the same company, your actions would become very predictable. Any terrorist who might be planning to do you harm would find this predictability helpful. Thus, the second rule for dealing with terrorism is, if you are in a high-risk situation or one where terrorist attacks have occurred before, become unpredictable. Don't go to or leave from the same places, over the same route, by the same means, in the same company, at the same time, for the same reason. You have the picture. After that:

- Stay unpredictable. Don't relax. Keep up your guard until you reach a safe place. Maintaining a state of crisis is not natural or easy, and therefore staying alert and attentive is something you have to work at.
- Cooperate with others who have responsibility for your security, such as those at airports and other public places. Don't interfere with their work, and don't try to beat the systems. If you can beat the system, remember that the terrorist can, too.
- Don't become paranoid, become prudent. Don't see

a terrorist behind every bush, but don't fail to look where you should.

- Stay out of places that proper authorities, like the Department of State, have declared to be dangerous.
- Plan ahead how you will approach a high risk area or situation. Get all the information you can, develop a game plan, and follow it.
- Stay flexible and able to respond to rapidly changing circumstances. Each situation has its own qualities and demands.

IF YOU SHOULD BE TAKEN HOSTAGE

On the remote chance that you are taken hostage, begin immediately to study the situation. Remember the first rule about being "psyched out." Don't let it happen. Instead, size up the situation, looking for details that will help you understand what is happening and, if possible, try to figure out what will happen next. In your head, map the positions of doors, windows or portholes, fire extinguishers and other safety equipment. Notice the dress, overall appearance, weaponry, and apparent mental state of the terrorists. You have been taken by terrorists and you could not control that, but you can control your own responses to the event.

The moment you have yourself under control, look around you to see if you might be of help to others. Don't make any moves at this point. The terrorists might not understand, and you could get hurt. But note conditions and be ready to help when that looks sensible. When you reach this point, you have fully taken charge of your principal asset for managing the situation—yourself.

Escape

In a hostage situation, some of your earliest thoughts may be of escape. Some hostages do escape. For example, Jeremy Levin, the Cable Network News bureau chief who was taken by Hezballah in Lebanon, says that he missed his first opportunity, and he was determined not to miss the second one. So when his guards relaxed their routine, he was ready, and he got away. As a second example, one time during the insurgency in Uruguay, the Tupamaros kidnapped an American diplomat, tied him up with rope and threw him on the back of a truck. As the truck sped into the country, he wriggled to the back and threw himself off. The kidnappers didn't see him fall off, and he got away. Moorhead Kennedy decided that the wiser decision was not to try. As he tells the story:

> Around the ambassador's residence where we were held, student guards would fire bursts with their submachine guns. We had no way of knowing whether they were just trying to scare off the mob outside the compound wall, or whether they were shooting the hostages one by one. My turn might come next, I thought. If that was to happen, then maybe I should try to escape. One night, I thought I had the chance. I slept next to a window that led onto a balcony. I remembered that an awning went down from the balcony to the patio around the pool, where I used to swim.
>
> Our guard would step out of our room from time

to time. Suppose I were to slip out the window, down the awning, and hide in one of the changing rooms next to the pool? After they had stopped looking for me, then I could run to the wall, clamber over it, and out to freedom.

But suppose, just as I was climbing through the window, the guard came back into the room. Suppose at the bottom of the awning, there stood a trigger-happy guard. Could I outrun these younger students, who exercised every day, to the wall? Suppose I reached the top of the wall. Outside, the mob was chanting "Marg bar Amreeka," "Death to America." Suppose they saw a real live American on top of the wall?

But if the students were going to shoot us, and if I hadn't at least tried to escape, wouldn't I feel pretty bad? Anyway, the students the next day moved me to another room from which escape was impossible.

Make the wisest choice you can given your particular situation. Weighing the odds and acting prudently could save your life.

DEALING WITH CRISIS SITUATIONS

The chances that you might ever be taken hostage are very slim. The odds are several million to one. But the things you might learn if you were a hostage would be very valuable to know, because they can help in dealing with many of the crises that arise in life, particularly those involving violence.

The statistics show that if you are taken hostage you are not likely to escape. Therefore, you may have to prepare yourself to endure captivity, and you will

Figure 21—When dealing with a terrorist situation yourself, all details about the surroundings should be watched carefully. This photo, taken November 17, 1979, shows demonstrators outside the gate of the U.S. Embassy compound in Tehran. Inside the Embassy, Iranian terrorists held Americans hostage.

have to learn quickly how you are going to manage that situation. Remember, though, that the survival techniques you learn must be ones that work for you. Other people, with different personalities, may handle captivity in other ways. With due allowance for those differences, you and anyone else in the situation with you will go through a series of predictable psychological stages.

Denial. Your first feeling may be, "This is not happening to me. This happens to those other people I see on TV, but not to me." That feeling is called **denial.** It is a natural reaction that will help you through the shock of finding yourself a victim of any violent situation, whether you are mugged, raped, taken hostage, or even caught in an earthquake.

Anger. When finally you face the reality that violence has hit you, not someone else, other feelings move in and take the place of denial. One is, "This shouldn't be happening to me," followed by, "If other people had been doing their jobs, this wouldn't have happened." You become angry, and you feel better for just a minute. Then anger will weaken you and make you less effective in managing your situation.

Quarreling or bargaining with yourself. Saying to yourself, "This doesn't have to happen to me,"is a form of bargaining or rationalizing. Like denial or anger, it helps you while you do it. When you stop, though, you feel worse than before.

During their captivity, one of Kennedy's roommates did this a lot, and as a result ended up crying frequently. He would ask, "What have I done in my life to deserve this?" He persuaded himself that because he was a good guy, nothing bad would ever happen to him. He didn't understand that bad and sad things can happen to you in life, no matter how good a person you've tried to be.

Fear. In captivity, with nothing else to think about, fear can hit you. Here are some of the symptoms—mostly signals your body sends you that something is wrong: Your body may give off a nasty odor, your heart may beat faster, your breathing may become rapid and irregular, your throat may feel dry, and your legs may twitch. You may find you cannot stand or that you cannot control body functions. That is fear; if it happens, fight it, but don't be ashamed of it. Some or all of these things happen to anybody under the stress of violent events.

Depression. **Depression** is feeling low in your mind and sometimes thinking gruesome thoughts. There are ways to beat back these feelings. If other people are also caught in your situation, try to cheer them up, and get them to cheer you up. As one of Kennedy's fellow hostages said: "We're all going to have to have our ups and downs. Let's help each other while we can." There are other things you can do to avoid loading on stress:

> **Keep fit.** Keeping yourself in good physical shape helps you to stay in good mental shape. If you don't have an exercise program, develop one and keep it up, even if all you can do is run in place.
> **Be careful about personal hygiene.** Personal care

is a great morale builder, so take care of yourself and the space you live in, and protect the equipment you have for doing that, like soap, toothbrush, towel, and so on.

Make effective use of your time. If you are confined for any reason, and you are physically able, try to keep busy. Ask for books, games, or playing cards. Ask for a pad and pen and write your own book. There is a famous Russian story about a man who made a bet with his brother that he could spend many years alone in a room. Over the years, the man thought, read, began to write, composed music. Finally he emerged, having won the bet, but he said it did not matter. He had learned one of the great secrets of living: how to use his own inner resources.

Looking ahead. The faster you develop and practice these and other techniques, the sooner you will be able to cope effectively with a situation which you can't change, or a future that you can't control.

PREPARING AT SCHOOL FOR DEALING WITH TERRORISM

The survival techniques we have just outlined are good for more than just dealing with terrorism. Throughout your life, you will be dealing with situations that seem out of your control. Perhaps you already have. However, following these basic guidelines can improve almost any situation.

Besides developing survival techniques, you can learn important ways to deal with international terrorism. As you have seen, international terrorists are usually of cultural, religious, national, or other backgrounds very different from yours. You may not be familiar with the factual background of a grievance that arose in a remote foreign country, possibly long before you or your parents were born. The psychology of those involved may be strange to you. As an outsider to a country and a quarrel, you may not be able to judge the extent to which this or that grievance should be taken seriously, and therefore, you are less able to think of ways to address it. Even though the terrorist may insist that you try, you may not be able to do anything about it.

Learn all you can about foreign cultures, the history and geography of other countries, and foreign languages. This will make you a more useful citizen and leader, because you will be better equipped to make sound judgments.

In looking at your own responses to terrorism or a government's response, think also about what each remedy might **cost**, in terms of lives, property, goodwill, territory, relations with other countries, and future opportunities. Consider, too, what we might hope to *gain* from each. The analysis that you will go through is the same kind, for example, that the Department of State goes through when it prepares recommendations for the secretary of state, the Congress, and the president. As you become more skilled at this kind of analysis, you will become a more effective citizen and leader, better able to form sound judgments about terrorism and about the many other problems, foreign and domestic, facing our nation. You will also develop a greater capacity to make sound decisions about your own life.

REVIEW QUESTIONS

1. If you were a newspaper reporter in a high-risk area, such as the Middle East, what steps would you take to avoid being caught in a terrorist incident?
2. Under what circumstances would you or would you not want to try to escape if you were taken hostage or kidnapped? Why?
3. What are some of the feelings you might go through if taken hostage?
4. What are some steps you can take to cope with the situation if you are taken hostage?
5. Could these be applied elsewhere in life? In other words, how does dealing with a terrorist situation teach you how to deal with other difficult, or "crisis," situations?

7 | **Summary and Conclusions**

You have seen that terrorism is a widespread and complex issue. Some of the terrorist attacks you have read about look more like ordinary crime, some more like warfare. How do you distinquish between them? You might have concluded that the kind of terrorism that intends only violence and destruction is more like crime, whereas the same act done for the purpose of overthrowing an unjust ruler, or in order to achieve independence, is more like warfare. Can you narrow this, and other distinctions you might think of, still further? What definitions have you arrived at?

This brings us to the first question:

- Why do terrorists do what they do?

We hope that you will have learned to distinguish the "public" reasons for terrorist activity, such as nationalism, religion/ideology, and ethnic/cultural identity, from the feelings and drives that also play an important part in the motivation of the terrorist. Always be skeptical of the labels that terrorists give themselves.

- Who are the terrorists?

By now, too, you should be aware that terrorism did not begin in the 1980s, and that terrorist groups operate in the United States as well as in foreign countries. Terrorists derive support from private donors as well as from governments.

- *How* do they do what they do, *where*, and *against whom?*

The risk of terrorism is worldwide. The means used by terrorists are various, with bombing used in about half of all recent episodes. In many cases, victims are chosen at random, among people who happen to have been on the scene. On the other hand, you were given reasons why terrorists deliberately target certain categories, diplomats, or businessmen, as well as ordinary citizens.

- What is the proper role of the media?

Terrorists use the media to publicize their causes. You should consider whether the risks involved in giving terrorists free publicity outweigh the importance in a democracy of giving enough information to the public for them to make informed choices. If you think that some terrorist events should not be reported in the media, then you will have to decide who makes that kind of decision, and according to what standards of judgment.

- When and how do we negotiate with terrorists?

You have learned to distinguish the kind of negotiation involving the immediate safety and welfare of hostages from negotiations leading to concessions demeaning to the United States, or providing incentives for future hostage-taking.

- Do the terrorists succeed?

Terrorists are often able to pull off attacks successfully, they can hurt or frighten people, and they get attention. Many get caught, if not always right away. In the long run, terrorist activity helped make possible the independence of Israel and Kenya. In many other cases, terrorists achieve no positive long-term results. Sometimes terrorists can change people's *behavior*, like the Americans scared off by terrorist attacks from visiting Europe. That did not necessarily make these Americans more sympathetic to the terrorists' causes. Most dangerous of all, perhaps, is the way terrorism might change the way we observe and protect people's basic freedoms.

- What are governments doing about terrorism?

On an imaginary trip to Europe, you saw examples of what governments are doing. We reviewed the way governments should examine terrorists' grievances, the usefulness of international agreements, and the uses of force.

- What can we do ourselves?

You looked at some guides to behavior avoid being taken hostage, and to deal with the situation if you are taken. What you learn by being in a terrorist incident or by thinking about one can be used in other difficult situations in your life.

As citizens of our country, you will be helping to shape opinion and policy on how we deal with various kinds of terrorism. People must care and learn about this international problem if it is to be eliminated.

One reason for terrorism is the belief of some terrorists that no one is prepared to listen or that people will listen only if their attention is seized by some violent act.

You must be prepared for the reality, however, that some may not want to listen to you. They may have made up their minds that the only way for them to reach their goal is through violence. In such cases, your first responsibility is to take steps to prevent violence, or to reduce its effects on people, institutions, and values. When innocent lives are at stake, or the fabric of our society is put in danger, the controlled use of force by lawful and competent authority, national and international, can never be ruled out.

So far, we have set forth ways of addressing terrorism in the short run. But terrorism is often a consequence of problems generated over a long period of time. To the extent that they are deep-rooted, we must develop strategies that may take a long time before they have any effect. Both kinds of strategies, long- and short-run, need to be undertaken right away, if we are to deal with terrorism's underlying causes.

There are numerous conditions in society that generate grievances. Some are frictions between communities that turn into animosities, like the Tamils versus the Sinhalese in Sri Lanka. Palestinians and Jews in Israel and historic Palestine, whether they have lost homelands or regained them, have longings which are very human and need to be served. And you can see examples of community frictions at home. A society and a world community work well when people listen to other people and when they are prepared to find nonviolent ways to handle animosities and grievances. When they do not, ordinary crime, or terrorist activity, can be the result.

Solving such problems usually means sacrifice, compromise, or concessions on somebody's part. And it takes leadership and cooperation from individuals and nations. Perhaps more than anything else, it takes patient and clear effort by you and others involved.

As you think about terrorism, keep in mind a basic rule. It is easy to have strong preferences and to be very upset when exactly the solution you want is not possible or acceptable to others. But most of our problems have several different kinds of answers, many of which will work. Many times the most important element in any solution to a problem is that people get together on it and work together to achieve it.

APPENDICES

In this section we will introduce some of the people who are actually involved with this issue. You will find out how you can get more information about the issue and how you can get involved yourself. You will also be introduced to a wise and friendly beast, a cool creature: The American Civic Animal. . . .

MIND:
An independent mind balances the facts and opinions heard by the ears with the feelings of the heart and soul and creates an independent opinion.

EARS:
Sensitive ears are able to hear the variety of opinions on every issue.

AGE:
Our scientists have recorded American Civic Animals active from the age of 7 to 107.

HABITAT:
The American Civic animal lives and participates in a variety of environments and climates ranging from voting booths to political conventions to study groups and soup kitchens.

EYES:
They range from deepest brown to brightest green to lightest blue, representing the magnificent diversity of American people.

MOUTH:
Big. The American Civic Animal likes to talk. However, for the mouth to make intelligent sounds, it needs to be accompanied by sensitive ears and an independent mind.

HANDS:
Sometimes big and strong, other times detailed and soft, the hands put the independent opinions to work, turning beliefs into action.

Activities:

Voting; reading; listening; organizing; demonstrating. It's quite difficult to narrow down just what American Civic Animals do. They are often spotted writing or calling their Congresspersons and representatives to keep these elected officials informed about what they feel. They have been sighted organizing summer activities for underprivileged youth and cooking meals for Senior Citizens who have trouble shopping for themselves. Perhaps you have seen American Civic Animals passing out leaflets at shopping malls, or singing songs at rallies. There are as many ways to participate as there are issues that need attention, and Americans eager to be involved. In the final examination, there is one trait that all American Civic Animals share:

American Civic Animals keep informed!

They often consume newspapers. Favorite national papers include the New York Times, the Washington Post, the Los Angeles Times and USA Today among others. Local papers also offer a wealth of regional information. American Civic Animals listen to television and radio news programs. In addition, they listen and talk with parents, teachers, coaches, sisters, brothers, neighbors and friends. Because without listening, learning and exchanging ideas, American Civic Animals can not wisely engage in one of their most fundamental and important activities: voting. If they can not keep informed, get involved or vote, they can not stay free. In a letter from one great American Civic Animal, Thomas Jefferson, to another great American Civic Animal, John Adams, Jefferson summed it up: "If a nation expects to be ignorant and free . . . it expects what never was and never will be." The American Civic Animal realizes that one can not be ignorant and free. The American Civic Animal gets involved first by keeping informed.

American Civic Animals are also joiners:

Observing the American Civil Animal 150 years ago, French author and traveller Alexis de Tocqueville said, "Americans of all ages, all stations of life, and all types of disposition are forever forming associations . . . of a thousand different types—religious, moral, serious, futile, very general and very limited, immensely large and very minute . . . At the head of any new undertaking, where in France you would find the government or in England some territorial magnate, in the United States you are sure to find an association." The American Civic Animals of today are just as apt to join organizations and associations as they were in de Tocqueville's time.

American Civil Animals often work with national organizations, but they also like to quench their thirst for involvement in a number of community oriented ways— such as neighborhood crime prevention groups, school support organizations, or environmental education programs.

The first step in becoming an American Civic Animal is to keep informed by reading a newspaper, reading a newsmagazine or listening to the television or radio news programs. What if you want more information? What if you want to become even more involved? The following sections will give you some specific next steps and some specific organizations.

HOW TO START

- Find the correct organization or individual: if you are interested in addressing the issue of poverty in America, the Foreign Policy Association probably would not be the best organization for you to contact. Similarly, if you want to let your Senator know what you feel about a balanced Federal Budget, for example, you must know his/her name. The best place to find out the correct organization and/or name is in your local or school library. The Book of Associations, which is usually in the reference section of a library, lists thousands of organizations and associations that deal with many different issues. Often the librarian can help you choose which one is appropriate for you. To find out the name of your Congressperson or Senator, one easy way to do it, is to call the Capitol switchboard in Washington, D.C. at (202) 224-3121. If no one you know can tell you the correct name, the operator who answers this number will.

■ Find the correct address or telephone number. After you have found the appropriate organization or individual, you need to contact them. This can be done either in writing or by phone. (Remember: Calling is more expensive than writing!) If the organization is local, check your local phone book. If it is outside your area, check for the telephone number and address in the Book of Associations. If you don't know the address or the telephone number, but you do know the town or city that the organization is in, call the area code for that city and then 555-1212. Tell the operator the city and the name of the organization and he/she will give you the correct telephone number. All members of Congress can be phoned by calling the Capitol switchboard at the number listed in the paragraphs above.

■ Write or call. Many organizations and elected officials are pleased to hear from interested people. Many are eager to pass out information or to get help from energetic volunteers who care about the issues they deal with. Many organizations, including both political parties and a citizens' action groups, welcome your participation. After keeping informed, getting involved is the next step to becoming an American Civic Animal.

■ What happens then? If you're calling or writing for

information, ask for the specific type you are looking for. If you want to get involved with the organization, it's best if you tell them you would like to volunteer your services. Very few organizations can afford to pay their young employees, although some organizations do. Most organizations will allow flexible hours to allow for school or other employment. What you end up doing depends on the organization. You might be speaking with people on the phone; you might write letters; you might deliver meals or translate languages. While the work is not always thrilling, being involved in an issue you care about and seeing the difference you make can be very exciting. And that can be a lot of fun. The next section describes some organizations that deal with the specific issues addressed in this book.

RESOURCES

Getting involved with the issue of terrorism is not as easy as it is with other issues, such as poverty, immigration, or drugs. There are no volunteer antiterrorist groups for the concerned citizen. However, if you would like more information than you can get from the newspapers or magazines or television, you could contact some of the organizations listed in this section.

United States Government Agencies

The State Department and the Department of Defense are two government agencies dedicated to stopping acts of terrorism. Throughout the world, from old terrorist hotspots, such as the Middle East, to newer terrorist centers in South America and South Africa, the Departments of State and Defense try to prevent and/or defeat terrorist acts. The Department of State publishes reports on different aspects of terrorism, such as a recent report entitled "Syrian Support for International Terrorism," and another called "Terrorist Bombings." These reports can often provide up-to-date and accurate information on the methods used to defend against terrorism and on the political turmoil surrounding terrorist groups. If you would like to get more information from one or both of these organizations, write:

The Department of State
Office of the Ambassador at Large for Counter Terrorism
Washington, D.C. 20520

or

The Department of Defense
Washington, D.C. 20301

The Department of Transportation, which oversees all American air travel, is charged with making our airways safe. During an average six-month period, 550 million persons fly from United States airports. The Department of Transportation is responsible for regulating airport security measures and trying to prevent terrorist attacks in the U.S. If you are interested in learning more about what the Department of Transportation is doing to protect civilian air travel, write:

> The Office of Civil Aviation Security
> The Federal Aviation Administration
> The Department of Transportation
> Washington, D.C. 20591

In Congress, the U.S. House of Representatives and the U.S. Senate both issue reports on terrorism and counterterrorism. The Senate Committee on Foreign Relations and the House Committee on Foreign Affairs release documents on different aspects of the terrorism issue, such as "AntiTerrorism Measures: The Adequacy of Foreign Airport Security," and "International Terrorism." All these documents are available through the Government Printing Office, usually for a small fee to cover the cost of printing. You can write or call them at the following address and number:

> Government Printing Office
> North Capitol Street
> Washington, D.C. 20401
> (202)783-3238

Within the United States, law enforcement agencies, such as the FBI and local police departments, cooperate to prevent terrorist acts. For example, the FBI stopped Sikh terrorists from blowing up an Air India flight from New York to London. Their investigative work saved hundreds of lives. In addition to the FBI, many police departments in big cities, including New York, Los Angeles, and Chicago, train special counterterrorist units. You could contact your local police department to find out how they cooperate with federal authorities to prevent terrorism.

Private Organizations

There are a number of private organizations which examine the issues surrounding terrorism and suggest ways to better control terrorism. These organizations are called "think tanks." These "idea factories," such as the Brookings Institution and the American Enterprise Institute, sponsor the research of scholars in a wide range of areas. The scholars, experts in fields ranging from human rights to international economics to Middle East terrorism, meet together with members of Congress, policymakers, business and labor leaders, as well as with one another to discuss policy ideas. The scholars then write educational and academic papers which the "think tanks" publish.

For example, in 1987 Brookings Institution scholar Christine Moss Helms studied Islamic politics and wrote a paper which focused on the role Islamic politics plays in terrorism and U.S.-Arab relations. At the same time, the American Enterprise Institute published "Terrorism: What Should Be Our Response?" the transcript of a television discussion featuring former Attorney General Ramsey Clark, and Yonah Alexander, Director of the Institute for Studies in International Terrorism at the State University of New York.

If you are interested in the research and publications of either the Brookings Institution or the American Enterprise Institute, write:

> The Brookings Institution
> 1775 Massachusetts Avenue, N.W.
> Washington, D.C. 20036

or

> The American Enterprise Institute
> 1150 17th Street, N.W.
> Washington, D.C. 20036

CURRENT POLICY NO. 667: COMBATING INTERNATIONAL TERRORISM

March 5, 1985, United States Department of State, Bureau of Public Affairs, Washington, D.C.

Following is a statement by Ambassador Robert B. Oakley, Director, Office for Counter-Terrorism and Emergency Planning, before the Subcommittee on Arms Control, International Security, and Science and on International Operations of the House Foreign Affairs Committee, Washington D.C., March 5, 1985.

Seeking to impose one's political will over others through the threat or use of violence is as old as history. Over the last few centuries, however, the civilized world was thought to have made progress in establishing nonviolent rules of political conduct. International rules of war, human rights resolutions, and, indeed, the fundamental premises underlying the establishment of the United Nations are all based on the assumption that political violence and political freedom do not, and cannot mix. Political intimidation, the object of the use of terrorism, is antithetical to freedom of political expression, the cornerstone of democratic society.

Sadly, there has been a growing trend in the past two decades by individuals, groups, and, in some instances, by governments, to resort to terrorism on an international scale in the pursuit of their political aims. In an age of high technology and mass communications such tactics are relatively cheap, effective, and produce a maximum of media exposure. They also cynically sacrifice the lives and well-being of innocent people and eliminate peaceful options of compromise and diplomacy. Left unchallenged, the rise of terrorism will undermine the system of political, economic, and military relationships which the United States and its allies have come to rely upon to preserve, protect and promote their national and mutual interests in an orderly and peaceful fashion. During the years ahead, we must be prepared for continued serious threats from international terrorism—in Western Europe, in the Middle East, and in Latin America, in particular—much of it supported or encouraged by a handful of ruthless governments. The challenge is clearly before us.

U.S. Efforts to Combat Terrorism

This background makes it clear that a tremendous effort is required merely to hold one's own, much less put an end to international terrorism, and that an international effort is required, not merely one by our government. No matter what our commitment and capability may be, we cannot succeed alone when the threat originates abroad and strikes abroad where other governments necessarily have the major responsibility. In this country, the leadership of President Reagan and Secretary of State Schultz and the strong support of Congress, particularly the House Foreign Affairs Committee, are providing both the means and the political will to combat terrorism. But unless and until other governments are willing and able to make the same commitment, the unfavorable trend experienced last year cannot be reversed. Without this international cooperative effort, the terrorists and those behind them will continue to be successful, which will encourage others to utilize terrorism to achieve their political and ideological goals.

We have strong leadership at the State Department in the struggle to oppose terrorism and improve security preparedness abroad. The Secretary of State has these subjects very much on his mind and makes clear daily to everyone in the Department of State that it must also be on their minds. He does the same for our ambassadors and diplomatic personnel abroad. He is leading a government-wide effort to promote international awareness and cooperation to address the common threat and convince them to work closely with us to counter, deter, and eventually end terrorism.

Under Secretary for Management Ron Spiers oversees and coordinates all this activity for the Secretary of State. Assistant Secretary for Administration and Security Bob Lamb; his principal deputy, Dave Fields; and I all report to the Under Secretary. While we each have our separate roles, we make every effort to coordinate our actions internally.

Assistant Secretary Lamb will address for you, at a future date, the overall organization of the State Department for security work. However, it may be useful to point out here that the Office of Security (SY), which is under his supervision, has the overall responsibility for the security of all official U.S. personnel, facilities, and, of course, national security information overseas—except, of course, for U.S. military facilities and personnel assigned to U.S. military commands. In addition, the development and execution of overseas diplomatic security policies are the responsibility of the Department's Office of Security. As Deputy Assistant Secretary for Security, Dave Fields chairs the Overseas Security Policy Group, which was formed in 1983. This group, composed of the directors of security from the major foreign affairs agencies, meets monthly to formulate broad operational security policies and to serve as a focal point for interagency overseas security activities.

The Office for Counter-Terrorism and Emergency Planning, known in the bureaucracy as M/CTP, has a traditional policy and coordinating role within the Department of State plus several more recently acquired responsibilities for administering State Department programs. These programs include: The Anti-Terrorist Assistance Program; Emergency Action Planning; and Exercising Embassy response capabilities.

As Director of M/CTP, I am also the chairman of the Interdepartmental Group on Terrorism (IG/T) established as a result of National Security Decision Directive 30 in which the President designated the Department of State as having the lead interagency role in combating terrorism. In this role, M/CTP is responsible for ensuring the coordination of activities by all U.S. Government agencies in combating international terrorism. The IG/T provides a very useful forum for the major departments and agencies actively involved in combating terrorism to meet regularly and share ideas, draw conclusions, and make recommendations on policy and programs. The permanent members include the Vice President's Office, the National Security Council (NSC), the Department of Justice (which has interagency responsibility for domestic terrorism), and the FBI, the Department of the Treasury, the Department of Defense and the Joint Chiefs of Staff, the Department of Energy, the Central Intelligence Agency (CIA), and the Federal Aviation Administration (FAA). Other agencies are invited when there is an agenda item of direct interest to them. The IG/T provides a single point to which the various departments and agencies can address questions and make proposals. The conclusions and recommendations of the IG/T then go to the NSC and the various agencies involved.

Goals of U.S. Counterterrorism Activities

Having noted the general nature of our activities, I think it might be useful to outline some of the goals which guide us in our daily activities:

First is attainment of effective coordinated action, both within the Department of State for Under Secretary Spiers and Secretary Schultz and among all the agencies of the U.S. government involved in combating terrorism.

Second is the effective integration between more passive measures for security and protection of our installations and people abroad and more active measures to deter or preempt terrorist attack.

Third is the attainment of international cooperation in combating terrorism. We believe that only through long-term, cooperative international action can terrorist problems be reduced. Because of the political realities facing us, such action often operates more effectively on a bilateral than a multilateral basis.

Finally, there is the need to utilize to the fullest our government's intelligence effort against terrorism. We recognize the importance of good intelligence in a form which can be assessed and put to use rapidly and, when appropriate, be shared with selected allies.

Effective Coordinated Action. Let me elaborate on some of our activities as they relate to these goals. The periodic crises which require our attention present good examples. What happens when there is a hijacking, a bombing, or a kidnaping outside of the United States? How does the State Department respond and how do we work with other agencies? Rather than set forth generalities, it might be more useful to cite examples.

When Kuwait Airline Flight 221 was hijacked to Tehran on December 4, 1984, the State Department set up a working group chaired jointly by my office and the Bureau of Near Eastern and South Asian Affairs (NEA). Other participants included the Office of Consular Affairs and the Agency for International Development (AID), once it was known that several AID employees were aboard the plane. This working group followed the developments of the hijacking in Kuwait and Tehran day and night until the last hostage was released nearly a week later. The working group coordinated actions within the U.S. Government, kept senior officials informed of developments, maintained contact with families of passengers, provided information to the press about the latest developments, and developed initiatives with other governments. When the hijacking came to an end, the working group organized transport back to the States for the released American hostages and initiated prompt debriefings in order that we might benefit in future incidents from the lessons learned.

At the time of the September 20 bombing of our Embassy in Beirut, the Department organized a similar working group which monitored events and coordinated activities around the clock. In addition, the Department of State sent two delegations to conduct two levels of inquiry. One delegation, headed by Assistant Secretary [for Near Eastern and South Asian Affairs] Murphy and which included representatives of M/CTP and SY plus other agencies, visited Beirut for 2 days immediately after the bombing for a quick survey of what had happened. Immediately upon their return, this team reported to the Secretary of State and the President on its findings. The second delegation, and Emergency Reaction Team composed of bomb and security experts led by the Department's Office of Security, spent several weeks studying all aspects of the bombing so that precautions might be taken at Beirut and elsewhere to minimize similar future threats. A full report was prepared covering all aspects of the situation. The activities of both groups were carefully coordinated.

The kidnaping of five Americans in Lebanon over the course of the past year presents another example of how we coordinate with other offices in the Department and other agencies in the U.S. Government. For most of the year, M/CTP worked on an almost daily basis with the Bureau of Near Eastern and South Asian Affairs to follow the latest developments, suggest to friendly governments and private groups initiatives aimed at the freeing of the hostages, and maintain contact with the families and employers. When news was received of Jeremy Levin's escape from his captors, the Department promptly organized a task force cochaired by NEA and M/CTP to be on the alert for intelligence and actions to take concerning the other hostages and coordinate Mr. Levin's release and travel back to the United States. In this and similar instances, there is constant communication between the State Department and other agencies and coordination with the NSC to ensure a unified position

Protection of U. S. Presence Abroad. We have taken a number of steps in recent months to improve coordination in security preparedness with our military commands and with private U.S. business and to see that what is done by these three major elements of the U.S. presence abroad is done cooperatively with the governments of the countries where they are located, whose responsibility is to provide protection.

To give you an example of the dialogue between the State Department and Embassies abroad on this aspect of our antiterrorism strategy, a telegram was sent by Secretary Schultz in mid-January to our ambassadors in Western Europe outlining the growing terrorist threat to the alliance there as seen by intelligence analysts in Washington. It instructed them to review the security prepredness of their own staff and facilities and also to continue and increase if need be their contact with U.S. military commanders and American businessmen, on the one hand, and with host government officials, on the other, in order to ensure maximum preparedness and maximum cooperation. Deputy Assistant Secretary of State for Security Dave Fields was in Western Europe shortly thereafter, going over security preparedness with his regional security officers, and his office sent out two detailed analyses of the country-specific and Europe-wide threats to U.S. installations and personnel. There was a subsequent preparedness coordinating meeting in Europe of officers from M/CTP and SY with the State Department Associate Directors of Security for Europe, Africa, and the Middle East, and with relevant U.S. military commands.

International Cooperation. In order to improve longer term cooperation with friendly governments, over the past

6 months, senior interagency delegations of our governments, including myself, have held personal in-depth bilateral talks with top-level officals in six friendly foreign capitals on the many aspects of this antiterrorist struggle, ranging from better intelligence and better physical security to more effective anti-hijacking measures and how to close legal loopholes which often allow terrorists quickly to go free and/or prevent them from being extradited. (This is also a problem for us, since several PIRA terrorists have been able to avoid extradition from the United States to the United Kingdom.) We have had a large number of discussions on terrorism with high-level representatives of other governments during the course of ordinary diplomatic exchanges. NATO foreign ministers at their December meeting declared their determination to suppress terrorism. Security of NATO facilities and personnel is kept under regular review in bilateral and multilateral channels. The heads of the seven governments that attend the annual economic summit address the threat of terrorism. At last year's London summit, the heads of state issued a strong and detailed declaration. Consultations, both bilateral and multilateral, continue in this framework. European governments are also addressing the terrorist challenge through the framework of the European Economic Community.

I am not free to go into detail publicly on these diplomatic exchanges. It is difficult to measure the near-term effect of such discussions, but progress has been made. It may be hard to prove this since the struggle against terrorism, even more than conventional warfare, requires secrecy. However, I can say that there have been a considerable number of actual or planned terrorist attacks against U.S. and friendly targets abroad which have failed over the past 6 months because of better cooperation among us in sharing intelligence and because of better preparedness and improved protection. I can also say that there promises to be still more improvement in both bilateral and multilateral cooperation—effective and purposeful cooperation—in the months ahead.

Effective Intelligence Efforts. Intelligence is clearly one of the keys to an effective counterterrorism strategy. But terrorism poses a special kind of challenge to the intelligence effort in terms of both collection and analysis. More than in any other intelligence field in peacetime, counterterrorism intelligence is action oriented. To be useful, it must be acted upon. Thus, there is often a hard choice to make between concealing our knowledge and taking advantage of it. In the past, there has been a tendency to protect intelligence, even within and between agencies, rather than promote its rapid use. Where lives hang in the balance, this is not an acceptable procedure. In addition, the bigger threat to our interests is from international terrorism, not domestic terrorism; therefore, we must rely heavily on other friendly governments, and we must be prepared to share information and analyses with them.

Interagency efforts to improve intelligence collection and coordination have included the following actions.

Terrorism has been made a collection priority for the entire intelligence community.

A 24-hour terrorism intelligence watch has been established at the Department of State and is in constant contact around the clock with other agencies.

At State, a special category of cables relating to terrorism with a special message caption now facilitates rapid, controlled distribution to all who need to know in the State Department and other agencies.

A coordinated interagency alert system has been developed to inform Embassies and other U.S. Government installations immediately of any threat.

CURRENT POLICY NO. 900: TERRORISM; THE CHALLENGE AND THE RESPONSE

United States Department of State
Bureau of Public Affairs
Washington, D.C.

Following is an address by John C. Whitehead, Deputy Secretary of State, before the Brookings Institution Conference on Terrorism, Washington, D.C., December 10, 1986.

I appreciate this opportunity to participate in this important conference on terrorism. I note from your program that you have already heard the perspectives of many distinguished academics and specialists; this afternoon, I would like to present our views on this scourge. More specifically, there are three questions that I want to address.

First, what exactly is terrorism?

Second, why is the United States so concerned about terrorism?

And third, what are we doing to combat it?

Let me begin with some observations on the nature of terrorism. In recent years, we have learned a good deal about what terrorism is and is not. What once may have seemed the random, senseless acts of a few crazed individuals has come into clearer focus as a new pattern of low-technology and inexpensive warfare against the West and its friends. And, while it is an alarming pattern, it is a threat that we can identify, combat, and , ultimately, defeat.

Terrorism is a sophisticated form of political violence. It is neither random nor without purpose. On the contrary, terrorism is a strategy and tool of those who reject the norms and values of civilized people everywhere.

Today, humanity is confronted by a wide assortment of terrorist groups whose stated objectives may range from separatist causes to ethnic grievances to social and political revolutions. Their methods include hijackings, bombings, kidnapings, and political assassinations. But the over-reaching goal of virtually all terrorists is the same: to impose their will by using force against civilians.

The horrors they inflict on the defenseless are calculated to achieve very specific political purposes. They want people to feel vulnerable and afraid; they want citizens to lose faith in their government's ability to protect them; and they want to undermine the legitimacy not only of specific governments but of the governments themselves.

Terrorists gain from the confusion and anarchy caused by their violence. They succeed when governments alter their policies out of intimidation. They also succeed when governments respond to terrorist violence with repressive, polarizing actions that alienate the authorities from the populace—and, thereby, play directly into the terrorists' hands.

Terrorism and Democracy

In thinking about terrorism, certain facts must be faced. All states and all political systems are vulnerable to terrorist assault. Nevertheless, the number of terrorist incidents in totalitarian states is minimal; markedly fewer acts are committed against their citizens abroad than against westerners. This discrepancy has not arisen simply because police states make it harder for terrorists to carry out acts of violence. It also reflects the fundamental antagonism between terrorism and democracy.

One reason that the United States is so concerned about terrorism, wherever it takes place, is that it is largely directed against the democracies—often against our fundamental strategic interests, always against our most basic values. The moral values upon which democracy is based—individual rights, equality under the law, freedom of thought, freedom of religion, and the peaceful resolution of disputes—all stand in the way of those who seek to impose their will, their ideology, or their religious beliefs by force. The terrorists reject and despise the open processes of democratic society and, therefore, consider us their mortal enemy.

States that sponsor terrorism use it as another weapon of warfare against the United States and our allies. Through terrorism, they seek to gain strategic advantages where they cannot use conventional means of attack. When terrorists, reportedly with Iranian backing, set out to bomb Western personnel in Beirut, they hoped to weaken the West's commitment to defend its interests in the Middle East. When North Korea perpetrated the murder of South Korean government officials in Rangoon, it sought to weaken the non-communist stronghold on the mainland of East Asia. When Syria participated in the attempts to blow up the El Al airliner and murder over 300 people, it attempted to strike a major blow against Israel, the United States, and Britain.

In Europe, the Middle East, and elsewhere, the United States is a principal target of terrorist violence, not so much because of what we do or don't do but, rather, because of what we are: a nation dedicated to the peaceful resolution of conflicts.

U.S. Counterterrorist Policy

What I have said thus far should give you a clear conception of this Administration's view of the phenomenon of terrorism. Now let me turn to the third and final point I want to discuss this afternoon: U.S. counterterrorist policy. I hardly need say that this is a particularly controversial topic just now. Many of you, I am sure, have strong views on this subject. Yet I urge you not to lose sight of the many real and substantial achievements this Administration has made in the fight against terrorism. Much of this effort receives little attention and takes place in the realm of intelligence gathering, in the cluttered office of analysts, or in the laboratories of scientists trying to develop better ways of detecting hidden explosives.

What are these achievements? During the past few years, we have made remarkable progess in thwarting potential attacks. Only successful terrorist acts receive front-page coverage, but I'd like to draw your attention to the attempts that fail—largely due to our efforts. Last year alone, we and our friends foiled more than 120 planned terrorists attacks. For example, in Turkey this April, security officers arrested Libyan-supported terrorists who were planning to attack the U.S. officers club in Ankara during a wedding celebration. In Paris, at about the same time, officials thwarted a similar attack planned against the visa line at the U.S. Embassy.

A number of initiatives have contributed to this progress. We have been developing our own intelligence capabilities vis-à-vis international terrorists and sharing that intelligence with other nations in a timely fashion. We have expanded international cooperation in the fields of law enforcement and counterterrorist training. Under the Anti-Terrorism Assistance Program, which began in April 1984, we have established active exchange and trading programs with 32 foreign governments.

States which may not actually train and fund terrorists, but which ignore terrorist activity in their own countries pose a particularly difficult problem. Unless their own citizens are the target of terrorist acts, many nations assume it's not their problem. We are responding to this unwillingness to act by discussing terrorism with all nations—not just our allies. I recently returned from a trip to Eastern Europe, which is an area well known for its leniency toward terrorists. Eastern Europeans are realizing that terrorism is their problem too: there were Hungarians at the Vienna airport when it was attacked last year, and Romania recently stated its opposition to terrorism. There is much more to be done in Eastern Europe, but with continued effort, we can make all countries understand that terrorism is a crime against humanity.

We are also for putting teeth into international antiterrorism conventions. For example, the International Civil Aviation Organization toughened its regulations dramatically after the hijacking of TWA Flight 847. In response to the Achille Lauro hijacking, the International Maritime Organization began to develop similar regulations for seaborne transportation. Last year, the UN General Assembly adopted a strong resolution declaring terrorism a crime, whatever the rationale.

We have taken great strides toward bringing our diplomatic installations in threatened areas up to the standards necessary to protect our people. All of our posts have conducted intensive reviews of their security needs, and these reviews have been the basis for speedy action. We have made immediate improvements at 23 high-threat posts. We are planning to construct new office buildings that will measure up to the latest security standards. The Inman Commission [Advisory Panel on Overseas Security] has estimated that improving the security of our institutions abroad will cost $4.2 billion over a 5-year period. Congress has approved less than $1 billion for the first stage. There is obviously a great need for increased funding over the next 5 years.

Our research into new technologies for enhancing physical security is also continuing. We have begun working with the private sector to help corporations improve their capacity for dealing with terrorists. We have passed tougher laws against terrorism, such as the Omnibus Anti-Terrorism Act of 1986, which makes terrorist acts against Americans abroad punishable in U.S. courts. And we are urging other nations to tighten their procedures for issuing visas to suspected terrorists.

We have also developed our own counterterrorist military capabilities to react swiftly to terrorist situations. In both the Achille Lauro affair and last April's assault on Tripoli, we demonstrated our willingness and ability to use force against terrorists and against states that support them. Col. Qadhafi now has no illusions about our determination—and neither should any others who would use terrorist violence against us.

Conclusion

Let me conclude with a final observation. Recent events may have raised doubts in some minds about the credibility of U.S. counterterrorist policy. But I can assure you that this Administration's overall policy is well in place, and it remains a sound framework for countering the terrorist scourge. Today, as in the past, our policy is based on four principles.

We consider terrorism a criminal activity that no political cause can justify.

We refuse to make concessions to terrorists.

We regard state-sponsored terrorism as a menace to all nations and promote cooperation among states on practical measures to track down, arrest, and prosecute terrorists.

We encourage international cooperation in isolating terrorist states to make it clear that costs will be imposed on those states that support or facilitate the use of terror.

Implementing these guidelines will not be easy. There are no magic solutions or quick fixes; and, as in all situations where human lives are at stake, there are political complexities and moral dilemmas that cannot be wished away. But, bilaterally and multilaterally, we are working at home and abroad in our war against terrorism. We are in this war for the duration, and we are determined to win.

TESTIMONY ON THE ANTI-TERRORISM TRAINING ASSISTANCE PROGRAM FISCAL YEAR 1988

Presented to the House of Representatives
Appropriations Subcommittee on Foreign Operations

by Ambassador Clayton E. McManaway, Jr., Deputy to the Ambassador-at-Large for Counter-Terrorism, Department of State, April 22, 1987

Mr. Chairman, thank you for the opportunity to appear before you today to discuss our budget request for the Anti-Terrorism Training Assistance (ATA) Program for fiscal year 1988. Appearing with me is Frank M. Fulgham, Director of the ATA Program in the Bureau of Diplomatic Security.

I propose to present for the record an overview of how the U.S. Government views the problem of terrorism, what progress we are making, and how the ATA program supports our efforts. I will then describe our current ATA activities and budget request for fiscal year 1988.

Summary

The Anti-Terrorism Training Assistance Program is an integral part of this country's effort to counter terrorism. Established in 1983 in consultation with Congress, the ATA program gives us an effective tool to enhance cooperation on terrorism with friendly countries. The program provides terrorism-related training and assistance to civilian officials of these countries which have acceptable human rights practices and face potential or actual terrorist threats.

While countries join this program for various reasons, including a desire to protect their own interests and citizens, there are benefits for the U.S. as well:

Most directly, U.S. citizens in the participating country, whether there privately or officially, as tourists or residents, gain a higher level of protection against terrorist acts than they would otherwise have.

The program facilitates regular contact between U.S. officials and those at the policy and working levels of the participating country. These contacts help foster cooperation and sharing of information on terrorism, itself a major priority for our counter-terrorist programs. All but a small fraction of terrorist attacks against American interests take place abroad. So cooperating with other governments is essential to our effort to combat terrorism.

When we work with a country to develop a set of procedures for dealing with terrorism, joint activities become more feasible.

A staggering proportion of terrorist incidents are directed against democratic states, many of them just beginning to emerge or reemerge after periods of authoritarian rule. Strengthening these democracies not only helps natural allies; it serves broader U.S. objectives as well.

It is not surprising that over 80 percent of terrorist acts occur in areas of importance to the liberal democracies. For terrorists despise most that which democracy cherishes most—respect for the individual and the rule of law. In many parts of the world, terrorism seeks to undermine democratic standards by calling into question the most basic government duty—the duty of freely elected governments to defend their citizens. And terrorism challenges the foundation on which our security is built, our respect for the rule of law.

COUNTER-TERRORISM STRATEGY

A review of the successes I mentioned indicates that while anti-terrorist measures—metal detectors, bullet proof glass, armor plate and the like—are indispensable, we must develop a strategy of counter-terrorism. We cannot protect ourselves solely by "hardening" likely targets. Our government must move beyond target defense to measures which will enable us to prevent attacks and punish those who carry them out.

We have therefore devised a five-part strategy of identification, tracking, arrest, prosecution and punishment designed to achieve this objective.

1. *Identification of terrorists is the first and perhaps most difficult step.*
   If we are to prevent attacks, we must know who the terrorists are, their origins, motivations and goals. Putting together this kind of information is difficult and requires close cooperation with our allies. We have in fact begun such cooperation in major areas with several of our allies. Our government, for example, has been compiling lists of known and suspected terrorists and has been circulating these "lookout" lists to friendly governments in exchange for similar lists from them. This kind of cooperation on intelligence sharing is absolutely vital to our counter-terrorism efforts.

2. *Once identified, terrorists must be located and tracked.*
   International borders are a weak spot for terrorists and an opportunity for us. In January, Mohammed Hamadei, who is accused of involvement in the TWA 847 hijacking, was arrested as he attempted to enter Germany through Frankfurt Airport. At almost the same time, another Lebanese terrorist was captured by Italian authorities while attempting to smuggle explosives into

Milan. We must also combat the fraudulent use of travel documents by terrorists. The USG is working now to make the travel documents we issue more secure, and we are cooperating with other countries to share information about false travel documents.

3. *We must act forcefully to apprehend terrorists.*

Because terrorists are far more dangerous than ordinary criminals, capturing them requires well coordinated intelligence. Crisis management experts and specially trained forces are also needed. Here too we have developed practical means of cooperation. Through the Anti-Terrorism Training Assistance Program (ATA), we provide training and equipment to nations trying to combat terrorism.

4. *The fourth practical measure is prosecution of captured terrorists, a step not taken often enough.*

Prosecuting terrorists in the face of terrorist threats tests political will. Recently, we have been encouraged by the action many countries have taken to prosecute terrorists in spite of these threats.

5. *Bringing terrorists to justice—punishing them—is the final step in the process of fighting terrorism.*

Merely thwarting them is not enough, for if the guilty know no fear, then the innocent can know no rest.

Fortunately, the rule of law is being asserted more and more. We see fewer terrorists released without trial. The Italians last year tried and convicted the Achille Lauro hijackers. In October and November, the British and West German governments tried and convicted terrorists for the attempted El Al bombing of the German-Arab Friendship Society in Berlin. In March, the French handed down a life sentence against Georges Ibrahim Abdallah, leader of the Lebanese Armed Revolutionary Faction (LARF) organization, for complicity in the killings of an American and an Israeli diplomat and the attempted killing of an American Consul General in Strasbourg. Other important terrorist trials are coming up in Madrid, Karachi, Ankara, Rome and Vienna.

These prosecutions must continue. There is nothing, no case study, no example, to suggest that there is any permanent advantage in treating terrorists as other than criminals.

This five-step strategy of practical measures is sound and is producing results. The ATA program is a key part of that strategy. Let me explain how.

THE ATA PROGRAM

The ATA program is divided into three parts. Briefly, these elements are:

Phase I. High-level officials of the receiving country come to the U.S. for policy discussions on terrorism-related issues and briefings on U.S. training facilities.

Phase II. A small team of U.S. officials travel to the receiving country to help design and develop an assistance program for the specific needs of that country.

Phase III. The actual training, is conducted in the United States.

In addition, the program sometimes offers seminars overseas on hijacking crisis management and document examination.

Current Program Highlights

While this basic structure has remained unchanged since the ATA program began, the program saw some changes during the course of fiscal year 1986:

Funding was increased from $5 million in fiscal year 1985 to the $9.8 million appropriated in fiscal year 1986, making it possible for us to expand the program. Eleven new countries began participating in the program. More than 4,000 officials from 44 countries have already participated.

Congress authorized spending up to 25 percent of total ATA funds to purchase course-related equipment such as airport security and communications equipment. This authority has enabled us to improve the program and help meet the urgent equipment needs of some participating countries.

We have developed and revised a number of courses, including:

- Airport Police Management
- Maritime Security
- Improvised Explosive Devices (I.E.D.) Render Safe

Although the program has continued to evolve, we have begun to see some specific progress directly attributable to the program:

In Latin America, ATA-trained personnel resolved a hostage seizure without violence. Similar situations had previously resulted in fatal violence.

In the Far East, ATA training and equipment were responsible for the greatly improved security of a major international airport.

In an Asian country, the ATA-trained dignitary protection unit provided excellent coverage for Secretary Schultz' state visit.

In a Mediterranean country, ATA-provided training, "bomb-sniffing" dogs, and equipment have been cited as being "critical to the safety of all airport users."

In a Latin American country confronted with bombings in the vicinity of embassies, we trained specialists to train bomb disposal squads and provided training and dogs for explosive detection.

The Fiscal Year 1988 Program

Based on a coordinated threat and risk analysis by my Office and the Department of State Bureau of Diplomatic Security, our fiscal year 1988 program priorities are to:

Continue to encourage the receiving countries to develop an overall coordinated plan for combatting terrorism

Train key supervisory, planning and training staffs

Continue to make the program available to countries that have both a need and desire to participate

Continue to evaluate, review and revise our training to make sure it is as cost-effective as possible

The fiscal year 1988 budget request covers the following program activities:

Executive Seminars (Phase I): $1,105,000. These senior level seminars normally involve eight to fifteen officials from separate agencies of the participating government who attend a two-week program of meetings in Washington and visits to anti-terrorism training facilities throughout the U.S. The meetings focus very heavily on policy issues. Up to 15 Phase I programs with senior foreign government officials will be conducted in fiscal year 1988.

Program Development (Phase II): $162,000. Phase II involves the return visit of a small delegation of U.S. officials who work with the U.S. embassy and host government officials to develop a program tailored to the participating country's needs. Up to 15 such visits will be made in fiscal year 1988.

Training (Phase III): $7,473,000. Actual training begins in Phase III. Courses take place in the United States and are conducted by a variety of organizations including federal, state and local governments, non-profit and professional organizations, and a few private companies. We expect to train some 2,000 participants in fiscal year 1988.

Equipment: $800,000. We anticipate using approximately $800,000 on training-related equipment (although this could change as we refine our assessment of each country's needs).

Program Management: $300,000. Program management funds provide for staff travel and transportation, rental of office equipment and supplies. The staff manages and coordinates all phases of the program, including presenting and explaining the program to eligible countries; developing and coordinating the Phase I Executive Seminars; participating on Phase II visits overseas; and developing and scheduling the training courses throughout the U.S. for participating countries; and conducting follow-up activities.

Conclusion

The Anti-Terrorism Training Assistance Program has proven its value in protecting American interests. Not only are more countries becoming involved, but, as our experience grows, we have been able to modify and add courses based on our earlier experiences.

The program serves our interest as well as that of the participating country. Countries participate for various reasons—including protection of their own citizens and interests. But a broad range of U.S. interests—including better protection for our own diplomats and private citizens—are served as well.

We appreciate the continued congressional support for this remarkably effective and, in our view, economical program. The cost of the world-wide ATA programs is $9.8 million—roughly a third of what our government pays for a new jet fighter. If the ATA training can prevent just one airliner from being destroyed in flight, the tangible economic benefits will far exceed the multi-year costs of the program. There is of course no meaningful way to put a price tag on the hundreds of lives which would be spared. But there is no question in my mind that the intangible benefits of a reduction in world terrorism are well worth the price and effort.

Thank you for your consideration.

GLOSSARY

anarchism/anarchist—the ideology that teaches that government is not necessary and not desirable. Anarchists believe in and practice anarchism.

arson—the burning of property in order to damage it. Arson is the second most common method used by terrorists.

concessions—something, or things—money, an airplane, housing, etc.—granted or given to another person or group. For example, the U.S. government might concede an airplane to terrorist hijackers in return for allowing hostages to remain alive. The government would not concede to other demands, such as releasing terrorists, who are currently in prison.

cost—the penalty paid. Every response to terrorism has a cost, in terms of money as well as many other things, sometimes even lives. When considering a response to terrorism, the costs of the strategy must be balanced against the gain.

depression—feeling low and poorly about yourself, and usually about your environment as well. Depression is one of the stages that many hostages go through, although it is important to try to fight it off.

dilemma—a situation where your choices are of equal value, whether good or bad. A dilemma often means that your choice is particularly difficult.

diplomat/diplomats—a person who deals with relations between two countries, working for one country while usually living in the other. Many *diplomats* have been the targets of terrorist attacks.

duress—pressure. If you negotiate under duress you are bargaining while under a lot of pressure. The pressure might come from many different directions—

you must negotiate the release of hostages before election day, you must keep negotiations secret, etc.

editorial judgment—a decision made by an editor regarding whether or not a news item will be printed. Editorial judgment is often exercised in controversial situations. For example, should the news of secret negotiations with terrorists be printed—yes or no?

factions—groups that unite against a larger body. Many terrorist groups call themselves "factions."

fanatic—someone carried away by enthusiasm for a belief or cause, to the point where he or she loses the capacity to judge objectively.

fundamentalists—in connection with Islam, persons who strictly follow the practices and beliefs of the religion.

guerrillas—in military usage, people who engage in irregular warfare.

ideology—the beliefs, ideas, and goals that make up a political, social or economic program.

imperialism—the policy of seeking to extend the powers or territories of a nation, often into areas distant from the nation itself. The Weather Underground reacted against what they believed was American "imperialism" in the Vietnam War.

intelligence—as in "intelligence" about terrorist activity— knowledge or information. These facts—such as where terrorists are living, where they get their money, where they are moving, who is in the group—are very important to the prevention of terrorist attacks in the future.

internal political structure—the different levels of government—local, state, and federal, that allow a country to operate. The internal political structure makes laws, sets government policy, and operates public services, such as schools, the military, libraries, etc.

Islam/Islamic—the predominate religion in the Middle East and much of Asia. Muslims, believe in one God, whose prophet was Muhammad.

media—when referring to news events, media means the methods of communicating the news to the public, primarily television, radio, newspapers, magazines, or books. Terrorists use the media to gain publicity for their actions and goals.

nationalism—feelings, such as affection, pride, or loyalty, about one's country or ethnic group. Also, the belief in its unity and goals.

negotiate—in terrorist situations, to try to come to an agreement over some matter—the release of hostages, the delivery of money, the return of a ruler, etc. Negotiations can take place on the telephone, through letters, through secret discussions, and in many other ways. How and when to negotiate with terrorists is a hotly debated topic.

nihilist—those who follow an ideology that teaches that traditional values and beliefs are without foundation, and that even our existence is senseless and useless. The word nihilism comes from the Latin word for "nothing," or "zero."

Palestine Liberation Organization (PLO)—grouping of principal Palestinian political and military organizations opposed to Israel, all of which use terrorist tactics in varying degrees.

psyched out—scared and intimidated so that you cannot act or react effectively.

publicize—to make known to a large number of people; to gain attention. Terrorists often use their attacks to publicize their causes or groups. Usually, the media—television, newspapers, magazines, etc.—publicize these events.

residents—persons who live in a certain area. Many countries are looking closely at their own residents—the people who live in the country—to try to find out who might have connections to terrorists.

Shiite/Shiism—one who belongs to the minority faction or branch of Islam. Those in the majority are called Sunni.

safehaven—a place where a person or group—such as a terrorist group—can live safely. Libya is considered a safehaven for terrorist groups.

supremacist—believing that a group is in all ways superior, or supreme, to other groups. The Order is an American, white-supremacist terrorist organization.

BIBLIOGRAPHY

ARTICLES

Andrews, James, H., ed. "The Iran-Contra Affair, Anatomy of a Quagmire." *Christian Science Moniter*, January 2, 1987,

"Beirut Bombing: Mysterious Death Warriors Traced to Syria, Iran." *Washington Post*, February 1, 1984,

Brady, K. "A Paris Court Stands Firm." *Time*, March 9, 1987,

Deming, A. "Fingerprints of Terror." *Newsweek*, September 22, 1986,

———"The Bombs of September." *Newsweek*, September 29, 1986,

Echikson, William. "Euroterrorists Are Acting Up, But They Aren't Acting Together." *Christian Science Moniter*, March 27, 1987,

Kennedy, Moorhead. "Lessons of Hostage II." *The Miami Herald*, June 30, 1985,

———. "Terrorism: Sources and Solutions. *The Humanist*, September/October 1986,

———. "Americans Held Hostage: The Moral Dilemma." *The Boston Globe*, January 5, 1987,

Newell, D. "Hostages: Cool It." *Newsweek*, May 18, 1987,

Powell, S. "Terrorism's Grim Upsurge." *U.S. News and World Report*, September 22, 1986,

Satchell, M. "Narcotics: Terror's New Ally [Special Section]." *U.S. News and World Report*, May 4, 1987,

Smolowe, J. "War on an Elusive Enemy." *Time*, October 6, 1986,

Thatcher, Gary. "New U.S. Data Showed Terrorism Ebbed in 1986." *Christian Science Monitor*, February 7, 1987.

BOOKS

Anzovin, Stephen, Ed. *Terrorism*. New York: Wilson, 1986.

Arnold, Terrell E. *Fighting Back*. Lexington, Mass.: Lexington Books, 1986.

Becker, Jillian. *The PLO: The Rise and Fall of the Palestine Liberation Organization*. New York: St. Martin's Press, 1984.

Grosscup, Beau. *The Explosion of Terrorism*. N.J.: New Horizon, 1986.

Gunter, Michael M. *Pursuing the Just Cause of Their People: A Study of Contemporary American Terrorism*. Westport, CT: Greenwood Press, 1986.

Gutteridge, William, ed. *Contemporary Terrorism*. Facts on File. New York: 1986.

Hart, Alan. *Arafat: Terrorist or Peacemaker?* London: Sidgwick and Jackson, 1984.

Jenkins, Brian M. *International Terrorism: A New Mode of Conflict*. Santa Monica, Calif. Rand Corporation, 1983.

Kennedy, Moorhead. *The Ayatollah in the Cathedral: Reflections of a Hostage*. New York: Hill and Wang, 1986.

Khomeini, Ayatollah. *A Clarification of Questions*. Translated by Resaleh Towzih al-Masael and J. Borujerdi. Boulder, Colo. Westview Press, 1984.

Kupperman, Robert, and Trent, Darrell. *Terrorism: Threat, Reality and Response*. Stanford, Calif. Hoover Institution Press, 1979.

Laqueur, Walter. *The Terrorism Reader: A Historical Anthology*. New York: New American Library, 1978.

———. *Terrorism: A Study of National and International Political Violence*. Boston: Little, Brown, 1977.

Livingston, Neil C. *The War Against Terrorism*. Lexington, Mass. Lexington Books, 1982.

McManus, Doyle. *Free At Last: The Complete Story of the Hostages' 444 Day Ordeal*. Los Angeles: Los Angeles Times, 1981.

Melman, Yossi. *The Master Terrorist: The True Story of Abu Nidal,* New York: Adama Books, 1986.

Moorhead, Caroline. *Hostages to Fortune: A Study of Kidnapping in the World Today.* New York: Atheneum, 1980.

Neomi, Gel-Or. *International Cooperation to Supress Terrorism.* New York: St. Martin's Press, 1985.

Netanyahu, Benjamin, ed. *Terrorism: How the West Can Win.* New York: Farrar, Straus, Giroux, 1986.

Pipes, Daniel. *In the Path of God: Islam and Political Power.* New York: Basic Books, 1983.

Raynor, Thomas P. *Terrorism: Past, Present and Future.* New York: Watts, 1987.

Rosie, George. *The Directory of International Terrorism.* New York: Paragon House, 1987.

Salinger, Pierre. *America Held Hostage: The Secret Negotiations.* New York: Doubleday, 1981.

Sterling, Claire. *The Terror Network.* New York: Reader's Digest Press, 1981.

———. *The Time of the Assassins.* New York: Holt, Rhinehart, and Winston, 1983.

Tahir, Amir. *Holy Terror: Inside the World of Islamic Terrorism.* Bethesda, Md.: Adler and Adler, 1987.

U.S. Congress. House. Committee on Foreign Affairs. *The Media, Diplomacy, and Terrorism in the Middle East: Hearing.* Washington, D.C.: Govt. Printing Office, 1986.

U.S. Congress. Senate. Committee on Foreign Relations. *International Terrorism, Insurgency, and Drug Trafficking: Present Trends and Terrorism Activity, Joint Hearings.* Washington D.C.: Govt. Printing Office, 1986.

U.S. Department of State. Special Report No. 149:*Economic Sanctions to Combat Terrorism.* Washington, D.C.: Government Printing Office, 1986.

How Much Security Is Enough? Current Policy Series, No. 923. U.S. Department of State. Report prepared by Robert E. Lamb. January 22, 1987.

INDEX